THE MORALITY OF
CAPITAL PUNISHMENT

Equal Justice Under the Law?

Michael E. Endres, Ph.D.

TWENTY-THIRD PUBLICATIONS

Mystic, Connecticut

Dedication

*To Erica and Heidi
and especially to Jon
for all his assistance and advice.*

Library of Congress Catalog Card Number 84-52707
ISBN 0-89622-224-1

Edited by Alice Fleming
Designed by John G. van Bemmel
Cover photo by Carl J. Pfeifer
Cover design by Kathy Michalove

CONTENTS

Chapter Seven
Morality and Law: Supreme Court Decisions   88

Chapter Eight
Morality and Law:
   Alternative Constitutional Approaches   **109**

Chapter Nine
Summary and Conclusion   **124**

INTRODUCTION

On January 17, 1977, Gary Gilmore was shot to death by the state of Utah. The firing squad that took his life ended a ten year moratorium on capital punishment in the United States. On December 7, 1982, the state of Texas held its first execution since 1964. This, the execution of Charlie Brooks, Jr., was in some respects a capital punishment watershed. The sixth person to be executed since the end of the national moratorium, and the first black person, Brooks was also the first person to be executed by the ostensibly more humane method of lethal injection. The controversy over a number of aspects of capital punishment was rekindled by the circumstances of Brooks's trial, conviction, and sentence, and the appeals process in the federal courts that eventually denied him a stay of execution. The Brooks execution and the "more humane" lethal injection method that accomplished it also raise the grim prospect of increased executions.

In October 1982, the U.S. Department of Justice predicted that executions would take place at the rate of two to three per week beginning in 1983. The projection was derived from the large, growing number of inmates consigned to death rows in capital punishment states, their average length of stay there, and the probable exhaustion of legal appeals and of other bars to execution. Other experts estimated more realistically that there would be 10 to 15 executions in 1983. Opponents of capital punishment characterized even this number of potential executions as a blood bath. Finally only

1

five executions occurred during 1983. The pace was picking up, however. In the first half of 1984, nine persons were executed.

The execution of Gilmore ended a decade of U.S. Supreme Court review of state capital punishment laws. Collectively, the opinions of the Court in these cases declined to find capital punishment to be inherently cruel and unusual within the meaning of the Eighth Amendment. Further significant movement toward constitutional abolition in the foreseeable future is unlikely. In December 1983, there were 1,202 persons convicted of capital crime, condemned to death, and awaiting their fates on the death rows of the nation. Two hundred and fifty-two persons were added to the death row population in 1983, a 15 percent increase over 1982. More are added every day.

Public opinion polls continue to reveal deep-seated fear of violent crime in our society. The great majority of respondents in poll samples support capital punishment, some vehemently. Since 1977 legislatures in many states have rewritten capital punishment laws to be in accord with Supreme Court guidelines. The issue of capital punishment would seem then to be largely foreclosed and accepted by legislators and the American public. Not so. Abolitionists, minority rights advocates, and civil libertarians continue to inspire a highly visible and real opposition to capital punishment. They are unlikely to abandon the cause under any circumstances. Significant numbers of politicians and members of the media and the general public are either opposed to or at least ambivalent about capital punishment.

In one sense, it was easier to support the death penalty than to oppose it during the moratorium. The ten-year absence of executions and their infrequency for several years before and after the moratorium led most Americans to indifference and complacency. But the threat of an accelerating rate of executions may reinvigorate opposition to the death penalty. Even those who marginally favor the death penalty may be averse to a blood bath. Furthermore, increased activity in the campaign against capital punishment can be expected when it becomes evident that highly visible multiple and serial murders and other homicides are unaffected by increased executions.

Aside from the matter of continued agitation on the issue of capital punishment, there is a more fundamental consideration. A truly humane society can never abdicate moral concern about questions related to the sanctity of human life. Whatever the policy, whether one of peace or war, of nuclear weapons and first-strike or retaliatory blow, of abortion, euthanasia, or capital punishment, the posture taken by the state is ultimately the responsibility of individuals in a democratic society. Nevertheless, we tend to take the morality of capital punishment for granted. Persons who are executed are presumed by their actions to have forfeited the right to live; they are considered the flotsam and jetsam of society. This position evades the basic question American citizens must ask: Is capital punishment good or bad, right or wrong? Is it just or unjust?

These are questions not often asked. It is the intention of this analysis to ask them, and to draw from the answers conclusions about such pragmatic issues as the cost efficiency of capital punishment and any number of other "good" results a citizenry that supports and institutionalizes capital punishment offers for its existence.

Answers are sought here to the most basic of questions: What kind of society do we live in? What does that society aspire to be? What role do our institutions play in helping us, as citizens, to create a decent human society?

Oddly, despite all of the rhetoric marshalled on behalf of either side of the capital punishment issue, the subject is seldom addressed in these terms. We are content to recite statistics at one another without inferring their greater significance. Our moral justifications are equally piecemeal. We hurl scriptural citations like thunderbolts in order to administer some theological *coup de grace.*

In the argument this book proposes, the fundamental insistence remains. If capital punishment is moral, it must be because it is a fitting punishment for humans when circumstances require it. If capital punishment is moral, it is because its use protects society with dignity and justice.

Capital punishment is not moral because of biblical code words or oversimplifications of scripture, no matter how sacred. It is not moral because it is cheaper (cost factors are morally neutral), or because vindictive public opinion stridently shouts that it is. Capital punishment is not even moral because the Supreme Court of the United States declares that it is constitutional.

What follows here is an attempt to examine capital punishment in a moral framework. The book argues that to be moral:

(1) capital punishment must better protect society than other alternatives; (2) it must better restore the order of justice and the solidarity of the community breached by the offender; (3) it must insure that innocents are not unwittingly executed; and (4) it must be imposed with scrupulous fairness. Data are introduced that verify that through the death sentence, none of these purposes of punishment have been or are now being met. Projection from past and present experiences and the analysis of social institutions lead to the conclusion that these purposes will not be achieved in the future. Therefore, this argument finds capital punishment can never be moral.

Augustine, Aquinas, and other earlier moralists could find no absolute theological or philosophical principle barring the death penalty. Neither does the argument presented here. Nevertheless, purposiveness and fairness are generally conceded as prerequisite to the moral application of the death penalty. Does capital punishment best serve those purposes proponents say it serves, and is it fairly applied to all who are condemned to it?

The format of the book is uncomplicated. In the beginning, it is necessary to provide a factual background against which the issues may be discussed.

Chapter Two summarizes a number of recent critical events relating to capital punishment in the United States. Chapter Two also considers both the benefits to society that proponents say result from capital punishment, and alternative approaches to capital punishment. It asks how some more humane approaches might better fulfill the purposes of a moral society.

Chapter Three explores the various acknowledged ways in which justice can miscarry, and observes how much less salvagable error is when it occurs in a meted out death.

Chapter Four deals with systematic defects in the operations of criminal justice. Implications are drawn from capital punishment in the future.

Chapter Five begins with the recognition that the deterrence of crime is a socially valued function of punishment. If it were clearly established that the death penalty is an effective marginal deterrent for capital crime, that it worked better than some other alternative punishment, a moral dilemma would be posed. Rights of individuals and social priorities would again apparently be in conflict. In this chapter and in Chapter Six, generalizations from deterrence studies are presented and analyzed.

The focus of Chapter Seven is on the relationship between morality and the law. Constitutional theories arising in recent Supreme Court capital punishment decisions are critically analyzed. Alternative interpretations, consistent with social values and constitutional principles, are presented in Chapter Eight.

Chapter Nine presents a reprise of the book and a systematic argument against the death penalty on moral grounds.

In sum, the reader is challenged to examine his or her ideological preconceptions, those values, beliefs, and social attitudes that bear on vital questions about the value of human life: What do you think of the prospect of a "blood-bath" on a broad scale, a return to what some have called legalized murder? Are crime and punishment reducible to some formula of exact justice such as that of "just deserts"? Is capital punishment itself reducible to a simple *quid pro quo,* an "eye for an eye, and a tooth for a tooth"? Is there a place for vengeance in the system of justice instituted by a civilized society that claims to be founded on Judaeo-Christian principles? Do we favor capital punishment or are we indifferent to it because those who are executed are usually not like the people we know, because they are considered the flotsam and jetsam of society? If the death penalty were almost exclusively for "solid middle-class" citizens, "respectable people," would we have abolished it long ago? What of respect for life as a seamless garment, as proposed by Joseph Cardinal Bernardin? Is it consistent to oppose abortion or war, yet be indifferent to capital punishment?

Those questions suggest only some of the issues addressed in the following pages. One's judgment about the morality of capital punishment should be knowledgeable and conscientious. This book is intended to inform and to stimulate the formation of conscience.

QUESTIONS FOR REFLECTION AND DISCUSSION

1. Discuss the relationship between capital punishment and public expectations. In what range would an annual number of executions satisfy but not repel the public?

2. What conditions of life are fundamental to a truly humane society?

3. Consider the essential role of fairness in the core values of modern democratic societies.

CHAPTER ONE

RECENT DEVELOPMENTS IN CAPITAL PUNISHMENT

Despite a ten-year moratorium on executions in the United States from 1967 to 1977, recent events manifest the continued awareness of capital punishment in our national consciousness. The allure of the death penalty is reflected in the escalation of favorable attitudes in recent public opinion polls and in the swift restructuring of constitutionally disallowed statutes by state legislatures. Prior to the Furman case in 1972 when the U.S. Supreme Court struck down the Georgia death penalty law, forty-two jurisdictions had death penalty laws. By the end of 1983, thirty-eight states had death penalty laws on the books.

Capital Punishment Abroad

The status of capital punishment abroad does not appear to offer any great solace to abolitionists. In a 1979 survey of over one hundred nations, Amnesty International found that only eighteen countries had unconditionally abolished the death penalty. Most abolitionist nations are in Scandinavia, Western Europe, or Latin America. France retired the guillotine in 1981 and entered the abolitionist column. A few other countries, notably Great Britain and Canada, have virtually abolished the death penalty, retaining it only for limited contingencies. At the other end of the spectrum, despite some tentative legislative initiatives in U.S.S.R. satellites such as Poland (pre-Solidarity and martial law), the communist bloc nations continue to provide the death penalty by law for a multiplicity of political and traditional criminal offenses. Albania is the only Eastern European nation that has abolished the death penalty. Very little headway has been made in the abolition of the death penalty in Asian and African nations.

Data on the actual use of the death penalty is quite inadequate for the bulk of those nations who still retain the sanction. In any event, such official data would be unlikely to reflect reality because in many nations of the world, including some in Latin America, summary execution for "political" crime is endemic.

U.S. Data

The data problem is not as acute in the United States, where reliable data have been collected for about half a century. With all respect for the U.S. Supreme Court's inference that capital punishment is *not* unusual *(Furman* v. *Georgia,* 1972), the actual use of the death penalty in the United States has been infrequent. At the time of the *Furman* decision in 1972, 42 jurisdictions, including the federal system and the District of Columbia, had the death penalty. Variations from that number in either direction were minimal in the period between 1930 and 1972. National Prisoner Statistics data, collected by various federal government agencies continuously since 1930, indicate that from 1930 through 1983 there were 3,870 recorded executions in the United States. This figure obviously excludes extra-legal executions. Lynchings were commonplace in this country, particularly in the rural South, into the early 1930s prior to the passage of the Federal Anti-Lynch Law. The 3,870 total does, however, include eleven persons executed in the post-moratorium period, 1977 through 1983. The annual number of executions has consistently declined from mid-1930s highs of approximately 200 per year. In the wake of favorable Supreme Court decisions on revised state capital punishment laws, the number of condemned persons on death rows around the nation has now risen to about 1200. As noted earlier, the outlook for the near future is grim. In October 1982, the U.S. Department of Justice was predicting a national average of two to three executions per week in the following year. Minimal projections were from 10 to 15 for the entire year. In fact, the actual number of executions fell far below even those much more conservative estimates. Opponents of the death penalty may be cheered by the limited number of executions, just as proponents feel frustrated by it. On the other hand, the continued highly selective operation of the death penalty should still concern opponents. And the acceleration of executions at the end of 1983 and early in 1984 indicates that there is always the possibility of worse to come.

The focus here is on the moral aspects of capital punishment; nevertheless, it is necessary to provide a legal and historic perspective. Therefore, capital punishment events occurring during the last decade and a half — an interval marked with unusual ferment on the issue — will be briefly reviewed.

Declining Support for Capital Punishment

Throughout much of the period between 1930 and the onset of the moratorium on executions commencing in 1967, homicide rates continued to decline (as had executions rates). Moreover, public opinion polls were indicating that attitudes toward capital punishment were softening. Indeed, as late as 1966, only 42 percent of the Gallup Poll sample favored capital punishment, as opposed to 62 percent in favor in 1936. (Recent polls report as many as 75 percent of respondents in favor of the death penalty.)

It is always difficult to assess the direct or indirect impact of global events on domestic issues. Post-war revelations of Nazi atrocities, culminating at the Nuremberg trials, stirred general revulsion against the perversion and punitiveness of German justice. Americans were repelled by the Germans' wanton disregard for the value of human life. (The Germans were quick to opt for *final* solutions to their perceived social problems.) It is quite probable that the horror and outrage created by such extremes had a temporary, indirect effect on American attitudes toward state-sanctioned death. Some credence is lent to that belief by similar temporary abatements of abortion and euthanasia as public policies.

The middle and late 1960s were times of social ferment, an era in which the spirit of liberalism walked the land. The Great

Society and its War on Poverty, the Vietnam War, and the anguish of the nation over its history of racism were no doubt at least indirectly reflected in the public ambivalence about capital punishment. Riots in the ghetto, and the confrontation tactics of political dissidents obviously intimidated policymakers and society at large. They were the stimulus for wide-ranging debates on American social problems, including issues of crime and punishment. Reaction had not yet set in, and it was unfashionable and untimely if not disadvantageous to buck the tide.

During this general time frame, the American Civil Liberties Union (ACLU), the American Corrections Association, and numerous other civic and religious organizations adopted official positions in opposition to capital punishment. The member nations also enacted United Nations conventions espousing abolition of capital punishment.

On the legal front, the Legal Defense Fund of the National Association for the Advancement of Colored People (NAACP) and the ACLU mounted concerted attacks on capital punishment, filing suits in state after state. The suits alleged that state capital punishment laws were in violation of the Fourteenth Amendment in their denial of due process of law and equal protection of the laws. Legal Defense Fund attorneys were successful in bringing executions to a virtual halt.

National Moratorium and **Furman *v.* Georgia**

Given the ambiguities in the stalemated situation, it was generally conceded that there were a number of issues related to the death penalty that only the Supreme Court of the U.S. could sort out. Finally, in 1972 in the case of *Furman* v. *Georgia,* the Court agreed to address those issues. It did so in its most comprehensive manner up to that time. Historically, capital punishment cases had been adjudicated on Fifth and Fourteenth Amendment grounds. Appellants alleged that their due process rights had been infringed by, for example, forced confession, the admission of tainted evidence, the incompetence of defense counsel, etc. Or they claimed that they individually were victims of discrimination or arbitrary or capricious actions; in short, that they had been denied equal protection of the laws.

In *Furman,* for the first time the Court attempted to broaden the basis for review of the death penalty. It attempted to bring it within the purview of the Eighth Amendment prohibition of cruel and unusual punishment, something which it had declined to do before. While the Court voted 5 to 4 to strike down the Georgia death penalty statute, it stopped considerably short of ruling that capital punishment was per se cruel and unusual within the meaning of the Eighth Amendment. Instead the decision held that the *operation* of capital punishment in Georgia was unconstitutional. The "jury discretionary" approach mandated by the Georgia statute left juries entirely free to determine whether to select the death penalty or alternative punishments. A number of the justices saw arbitrary, unfair applications resulting from the defects of the statute.

The major problem presented by the *Furman* decision was that each of the nine justices felt compelled to write a separate opinion, either in concurrence or dissent. Some who agreed to strike down the Georgia statute, notably Justices Marshall and Brennan, would have gone further to hold capital punishment to be cruel and unusual on more universal grounds. Yet, as the opinions of the other justices in the *Furman* case indicate, and as the ruling in *Gregg* v. *Georgia* five years later confirms, the thrust of *Furman* was minimal. It was directed at the application of capital punishment — the defects of the statute itself.

The States Respond to **Furman**

In response to the *Furman* decision, legislatures in Georgia, Florida, and other states, re-enacted "guided discretionary" statutes. The criminal trial was split into guilt determination and penalty assessment phases. Juries were required to consider evidence of mitigating and aggravating circumstances (defined in the statutes) in deciding on the death penalty on conviction of a capital felony. A number of other states eventually rewrote their death penalty laws in emulation of the still-to-be-tested Georgia model. Still other states had, however, read the message of *Furman* quite differently. In response to the Supreme Court's condemnation of arbitrariness, they opted to deprive sentencing judges or juries of all discretion. Their approach was simply to make the death penalty mandatory (automatic) for all capital offenses.

Supreme Court Review of Revised Statutes

The scene was then set for a series of critical decisions in a number of key companion cases decided in 1976. In the *Gregg, Proffitt,* and *Jurek* cases the death penalty laws of Georgia, Florida, and Texas were sustained on the grounds that juries were "guided" in their exercise of discretion by statutory limits. In short, such statutes eliminated arbitrary action and thus could not be judged to be cruel and unusual in applying capital punishment. At the same time, in the *Woodson* and *Roberts* cases, the Court struck down mandatory death penalty laws in North Carolina and Louisiana on the grounds that they did not permit juries the opportunity to take into account aggravating and mitigating circumstances in arriving at their decisions. This failure apparently rendered the statutes cruel and unusual and in violation of the Eighth Amendment. In brief, these rulings along with that in *Furman* in 1972 reached two conclusions. First, the death penalty is not inherently cruel and unusual within the meaning of the Eighth Amendment to the U.S. Constitution, but may in its mode of application be cruel and unusual. Second, those statutes may pass constitutional muster that *permit but guide* the discretion of judge or juries. Mitigating and aggravating circumstances surrounding the criminal act are to be weighed in the decision. In this manner, arbitrariness is to be excluded.

Subsequently, in 1977 in *Coker* v. *Georgia,* the Supreme Court reviewed the Georgia death penalty statute again. This time it overturned a section of the statute that provided the death penalty for rape of a woman. The decision of the Court held that the death penalty was cruel and unusual in this case in that it was disproportionate to the gravity of the crime. Finally, in 1982, the Court ruled in *Enmund* v. *Florida* that the death penalty for a "nontriggerman" accomplice in a murder committed while otherwise engaging in a felony (so-called felony murder) is also excessive. It is, therefore, cruel and unusual and proscribed by the Eighth Amendment.

Significance of **Furman** *and Related Cases*

Ostensibly, *Furman, Gregg,* and related capital punishment cases were decided on Eighth Amendment cruel and unusual grounds. Indeed, the justices generally used the language of the Eighth Amendment in dissenting as well as concurring in these cases. Nevertheless,

Frederic C. Rieber and other students of capital punishment issues have argued that whatever the rubric specified or the language used, the issues really addressed and the rationales that are relied on are essentially those of the Fifth and Fourteenth, not the Eighth Amendment. In other words, the cruelty or unusualness of the death penalty were never really at issue. Questions related to the *character* of the penalty itself were never discussed. Thus, for example, the mode of execution was never a consideration in *Furman, Gregg,* or any of the modern death penalty cases. There was no consideration of whether or not the death penalty inflicted pain "wantonly or unnecessarily," or that it was repugnant to human dignity.

Furman, Gregg, and related cases established that in order to forestall arbitrary decisions, the discretion of judges or juries had to be limited by guidelines. Specifically, aggravating and mitigating circumstances surrounding the crime had to be considered in determining a punishment. Relatedly, *Woodson* v. *North Carolina* ruled out mandatory death penalty laws which would have denied all choice to judge or juries. All of these cases dealt with purely *procedural* questions. Thus, in the *Furman* case, the justices actually found the Georgia statute unconstitutional because it permitted arbitrary, unfair procedures. In reality, the statute appeared to have violated the Fifth and Fourteenth Amendments which guarantee due process of law (including among other things, fair procedures). Otherwise, his colleagues might have followed Justice Douglas's lead and found that the Georgia statute also discriminated against black defendants. In that case, they might also have found the statute unconstitutional on the grounds that it denied equal protection of the laws, also forbidden by the Fourteen Amendment. They did neither. Instead, they achieved a curious result. While they generally argued the issue in terms of unfair procedures or discrimination, they concluded that the death penalty as applied in Georgia was cruel and unusual and thus in violation of the Eighth Amendment. The Fourteenth Amendment's requirements of due process and equal protection were all but forgotten. On the grounds of logic and language, arbitrary or discriminatory application of a penalty is certainly more repugnant to due process and equal protection than they are cruel and unusual.

On the other hand, the *Coker* and *Enmund* decisions might be better fitted into the framework of cruel and unusual. Respectively, those cases dealt with capital punishment for rape, and for a "nontriggerman" accomplice in felony murder. In both cases, the Supreme Court decided that the death penalty was cruel and unusual and thus unconstitutional because it was disproportionate to the gravity of the crime. It is certainly cruel to inflict pain wantonly or needlessly, as the Supreme Court has consistently held. It is also cruel to inflict more pain or punishment than is merited by the crime. In these cases, it was logical then to conclude that the death penalty was cruel and unusual. This distinction between the language and rationales used in deciding recent capital punishment cases has practical significance. Other arguments that might render capital punishment per se cruel and unusual will be considered later. Other due process and equal protection grounds that the Court might have relied on will also be discussed.

Ambivalence in Society

For now, it is sufficient to note that the Court's decisions reflect the uncertainty, ambivalence, and conflict about the death penalty that characterize American society as a whole. Fears about rising rates of violent crime, sympathy for victims and their survivors, notions about exact justice, and desires for retribution struggle with humanitarian sensibilities, a civilized abhorrence of calculated violence, even under the aegis of the state, and recognition of the enormity and irrevocability of the penalty. Indeed, as Mr. Justice Stewart suggested in his opinion for the Court in the *Gregg* case, the infrequent use of the death penalty in our own time may well be indicative of a civilized concern for the value of human life.

Future of Death Penalty Issue

It is difficult to foresee what impact, if any, more frequent executions will have on American attitudes toward the death penalty in the near future. Public opinion is highly volatile, and attitudes toward capital punishment have proven to be susceptible to short run influences by many variables. It does not appear likely, however, that there will be further movement toward abolition of the death penalty. Legislative bodies have continued to bring the death penalty back. In fact, in 1983 the Massachusetts legislature re-established the death penalty after the state supreme court virtually declared the existing statute unconstitutional on the grounds that capital punishment was cruel and unusual; earlier the California legislature had done the same. A strong but unsuccessful effort was mounted to enact a death penalty statute in the traditionally abolitionist state of Michigan. Recent attempts have also been made in Oregon. It does not appear likely that judicial review will further curtail capital punishment in the way that the cases in the 1970s and the early 1980s did. The more conservative complexion of the U.S. Supreme Court, further augmented by the retirement of the "swing man" Justice Potter Stewart, and his replacement by Justice Sandra Day O'Connor appears to preclude liberal movement in the foreseeable future.

In sum, the situation is this. States have been able to rewrite death penalty laws in substantial conformity to constitutional requirements as defined by the U.S. Supreme Court. It is unlikely that further substantial restrictions on the death penalty will be forthcoming from either legislative or judicial sources. The moratorium ended with the execution of Gary Gilmore in 1977 and several other persons since then. Meanwhile, the population of condemned persons on death rows swells daily. As appeals are exhausted in the forthcoming months, executions will begin all over again on a broader scale.

Unresolved Issue

The capital punishment issue is far from resolved. The legalities involved are not inconsequential, but they are not at the heart of the issue. Constitutional interpretations of social issues have proven historically to be largely reactive; they tend to respond to changing social conditions and social mores. Witness, for example, the radical alteration of the constitutional law on race relations as social attitudes have gradually changed. In *Plessy* v. *Ferguson* in 1896, the Supreme Court legitimated the black/white compartmentalization of almost every area of life when it enunciated the separate but equal doctrine. In 1954, in *Brown* v. *The Board of Education of Topeka, Kansas,* the famous school desegregation case, the Court took a major step in eliminating the barriers built up between the races.

Various constitutional law scholars estimate the number of overturned Supreme Court precedents over the years at somewhere between 150 and 200. At the core of the capital punishment issue are fundamental moral questions—questions of goodness or badness, rightness or wrongness—questions which the law is about but which transcend the law itself. It is interesting to note, for example, that even apparently more painless and more humane methods of execution can lead to protracted moral and ethical divisions. In the sequel to the first American execution by lethal injection, the role of a physician—employee in the Texas Correctional System in the execution was submitted to intensive scrutiny and criticism. In fact, the state of Idaho was among the first to adopt the lethal injection method in 1978. In 1982, without having yet carried out an execution under that legislation, the state legislature authorized and funded a standby method of execution by firing squad. The legislature feared that the objections of the medical profession and other interested groups would hamstring the lethal injection method. The lethal injection method continues to run into difficulty. After earlier attempts to resolve the matter in the lower courts, the U.S. Supreme Court has agreed to decide in its 1984-1985 term whether or not the states may utilize various chemicals in lethal injections without prior FDA testing and approval of their safety and effectiveness.

Ultimately, the capital punishment issue is a moral issue and thus the criteria of judgment are not pragmatic but moral. In its broadest terms the question inherent in the death penalty debate may be stated in imperative terms: What kind of society should this be— what kind of society do we choose to dwell in? The enormity of that issue argues against an easy resolution, or any lengthy hiatus in the recurring disquiet that we experience over the death penalty. Neither retention of the death penalty in any number of states, and an accelerated rate of execution, nor total abolition for that matter, permit the issue to evaporate.

QUESTIONS FOR REFLECTION AND DISCUSSION

1.   Relate the use of the death penalty for "political crimes" and traditional crimes to the value that a society places on human life.

2. In the U.S., the 1960s and 1970s were characterized by widespread political dissent and a perceived permissiveness. To what extent, if any, do the contemporary emphasis on law and order, and favor toward the death penalty illustrate a reaction to the perceived excesses of that period?

3. Contrast the strengths and weaknesses of the "guided discretionary" and "mandatory" approaches to imposing the death penalty.

4. Identify the relationship between morality and law in society. Point up the similarities and differences between moral and legal norms.

5. Does the mode of lethal injection dignify the process of execution?

6. Discuss the eventual impact of the outcome of the 1984 presidential election on the composition of the U.S. Supreme Court and future rulings on death penalty issues.

CHAPTER TWO

MORAL FRAMEWORKS AND CAPITAL PUNISHMENT

This book opposes capital punishment on moral grounds. Consequently, the focus is on arguments against the death penalty. Not that the arguments of proponents are morally neutral. On the contrary, their moral implications must also be considered, since one can hardly argue effectively on one side of an issue while ignoring conflicting assertions. The death penalty as it exists, however, is of ancient origins and continues to command broad support. Therefore, those who would contest it must perforce bear the burden of repudiation.

This chapter is concerned with arguments on two levels. The first and most fundamental level centers on the purposes of punishment and the relationship of capital punishment to those purposes. A related set of arguments, conveniently classified as theological, humanitarian, and pragmatic is also considered here. Later in the chapter, these classes will be identified and pro and con arguments will be presented and weighed. Their bearing on the moral legitimacy of capital punishment will then be evaluated.

Purposes of Punishment

The first requirement in evaluating the morality of capital punishment is to identify its purposes or objectives. Indeed, whether or not a punishment is initially legal depends upon whether or not it serves a valid goal or purpose of public policy. Obviously, the individual cannot be caused pain or his rights limited to no good purpose. Likewise, a punishment that inflicts harm on the person can hardly be good or moral if it is purposeless. Therefore, the first consideration in this chapter is to identify the purposes of punishment and to determine how effectively the death penalty serves any of them.

Any form of punishment may be imposed upon the wrongdoer for one or a combination of the following purposes: (1) to protect the community from recidivism by this particular offender (special deterrence), or from criminal offenses by others who may profit by the example (general deterrence); (2) to rehabilitate the offender; and (3) to restore the moral order breeched by the violation of community norms and the rights of others. As the following discussion shows, capital punishment is not required by any of the general purposes of punishment. Other alternatives may serve better or as well.

Rehabilitation of the Offender   In one case, the death penalty is clearly counterproductive. The second purpose, the rehabilitation of the offender, is obviously inapplicable in the case of capital punishment. The death penalty is no more recuperative in either a social or personal sense than would be the deliberate termination of life in a cancer patient. The American Cancer Society would hardly define the latter form of remission to be a success or cure.

Incapacitation   There is not much question about the death penalty's service in the cause of special deterrence. It is incontestable that the execution of an offender is the most certain way to incapacitate him or eliminate his further offenses against society.

The death penalty is not, of course, the only way to achieve this end. For example, lengthy periods of incarceration may effectively incapacitate the offender when it is necessary to do so. Moreover, other criteria must be considered in judging the fitness of the death penalty. While death may be the most certain prevention, it is also the most extreme. There is some uncertainty in prolonged incarceration or life terms which permit eventual parole; admittedly some statistically small risk of serious reoffending exists. At the same time, there is also a statistically small risk of executing a person who is innocent of serious wrongdoing. There is also a *substantial* risk of executing guilty persons *unjustly*.

The discretion permitted officials in the criminal justice system generates disparities. This occurs, for example, when pleas are negotiated for reduction of sentence with one or more accomplices in a murder, while imposing the death penalty on one or more of the others. This was exactly what happened to Charlie Brooks, Jr. who was executed in 1982 in the state of Texas. Brooks and his lone accomplice were charged with murder in the commission of another felony, defined as aggravated murder under Texas law. Consequently they were both eligible for the death penalty. Neither Brooks nor his accomplice would ever admit to being the triggerman. And the state was never able to clearly establish the triggerman's identity. Still, Brooks's accomplice was sentenced to 40 years in prison as a result of an eventual plea bargain; Brooks was sentenced to death by lethal injection. Despite desperate legal efforts on his behalf (ironically, including those of the prosecutor who had originally tried his case), the federal appellate courts refused to rehear the merits of his appeal. Finally, when the U.S. Supreme Court refused an eleventh hour stay of execution, time ran out for Charlie Brooks. The Supreme Court's refusal to block the Brooks execution has an irony of its own. At the end of its 1982 summer term, the Court had ruled in the case of *Enmund* v. *Florida* that the death penalty was disproportionately severe for a nontriggerman accomplice in such felony murders and was thus cruel and unusual under the Eighth Amendment. Since it was never established whether it was Charlie Brooks or his accomplice who had actually committed the murder, it would seem that the Court should have had little hesitancy about staying his execution and hearing the merits of his appeal.

There are other, less flawed ways to incapacitate dangerous offenders, if we have the will to use them. For example, life imprisonment without possibility of parole is a realistic alternative for the small number of offenders who are likely to be executed in any given year. And it carries absolutely no risk to the community. Moreover, life imprisonment does not risk irredeemable miscarriages of justice or extenuate inequities that may be created by the malfunctions of the criminal justice system. These matters are considered at greater length in the concluding chapter. At present, it is sufficient to note that there is no indispensability about the final solution.

General Deterrence   The purpose of general deterrence is no doubt the most applicable to capital punishment. If the state may, by taking the life of the grievous offender, deter others from similarly harming the community, the extreme penalty of death might appear to be warranted. In principle, the community's right and obligation to protect the innocent might take priority over the rights of the guilty. Some would still oppose the death penalty on absolute grounds, independent of any purported deterrent effect. For most opponents of capital punishment, the crux of the problem is, however, deterrence. To say that some punishment is justified by this purpose is not the same as saying that the extreme of capital punishment is justified because it does deter. Another qualification on the death penalty as a deterrent has recently been indirectly addressed by the Supreme Court. In ruling that the death penalty was excessive and unconstitutional for the crimes of rape and accomplice to felony murder, the Court recognized the first principle of deterrence: excessive penalties are not acceptable. In analogous terms, a nation has no right to deter other potential aggressors by punishing an enemy in a conventional war with a first strike nuclear attack.

Another implicit aspect of the death penalty as a deterrent is frequently overlooked: there are always alternative pathways to similar ends. The question becomes then, what is the most effective deterrent among alternative punishments? In other words, what must really be determined about the death penalty is whether or not is is *marginally* deterrent. To what extent does the death penalty prevent targeted crimes more effectively than alternatives such as life imprisonment? Opponents of capital punishment would generally be unwilling to concede that capital punishment has social utility if it is not established that it is a superior deterrent. The question of the marginally deterrent effect of capital punishment is merely posed here in relationship to the purposes of punishment. Separate chapters focus on capital punishment and deterrence and the question is answered there.

Restoration of the Moral Order and an Order of Justice   Perhaps the most complicated of all of the purposes of punishment is that of restoring the moral order and the order of justice.

There are two related, but qualitatively distinct interpretations that could be given to this purpose. On one side, there are motives inspired by the emotional elements in human nature. There is the primordial urge to lash back at an offender, the natural tendency to return pain for pain received. Such reactions are basic to clan justice, for example, the *lex talionis* of the Old Testament. Collective punishments, including the capital kind, are frequently rationalized on such grounds. It is often argued that when the community is unwilling or unable to control crime through the imposition of stringent penalties, the individual is encouraged to take the law into his own hands. In fiction, personal avengers and vigilantes are depicted as deriving deep-seated emotional satisfaction in meting out just deserts to malefactors. Readers or audiences respond with similar feelings. No doubt the sometime popularity of capital punishment in American public opinion reflects the ebb and flow of such emotional needs.

Opponents of capital punishment tend to dismiss such retributive motives out of hand, to condemn them as primitive and animalistic. On the other hand, there are compelling considerations of justice which ought not to be lightly dismissed. If justice is essentially fairness, we are required to ask, is it fair that one profits from another's loss? Should we not feel it grossly unfair when innocent life is taken to gratify the needs of the slayer for economic gain, power, vengeance, or whatever? Quite aside from the need to protect society, doesn't the offender *owe* something to those who survive the victim—to family, to friends, to the community as a whole? Thus, in whatever form, punishment may also be seen as compensatory. In the civil law of torts, judgments are rendered and penalties imposed on one individual or party in behalf of another individual or party. Under the criminal law, the obligation of the offender is to the community as a whole, aside from any additional responsibilities which may be imposed on behalf of the victims or their kin.

There is a related matter of no small importance. Society is a moral unity. It is a system of social interactions which binds us to one another. An offense by one harms the well-being of all. Life in human society would be impossible if we could not have reasonable expectations of one another. While we can never afford to be naive and must always be wary of others, particularly when we do not know them, neither can we live together without a fundamental level of trust. The butcher, the baker, the druggist must be able to exchange their commodities without fear of adulteration or tainting by uncleanliness or poison. No matter how defensively he drives, the motorist must believe that people will not drive cars when they have had too much to drink, or that people will obey traffic signals. The alternatives to mutual trust and mutual expectations are alienation and paralysis. Life in human society would be impossible if one could violate the law with impunity. In part, the criminal law exists to reaffirm our need and our ability to depend on one another. Collective sanctions exist, therefore, not only to incapacitate or deter or rehabilitate the offender. They also exist to restore a moral unity uninterrupted by violations of trust and to be sure the offender atones for his wrongdoing. Indeed, without this dynamic, the rehabilitative purpose of punishment would lose its meaning. Individual reform is the flip side of the requirement to compensate others in some way for that which has been taken from them.

Note that semantic arguments about what constitutes punishment are avoided here. Penalties of whatever kind imposed by the criminal courts are punishments. Neither the wisdom nor the efficacy of particular punishments (e.g., probation and restitution versus incarceration for property crimes) are being discussed at present. What is of concern now is the legitimacy of punishment in the interests of justice and the moral solidarity which binds us to one another. Such interests ought to be assigned to the more primitive level and dismissed as simply vengeful.

Vengeful motives for the death penalty ought to be repudiated. They emanate from the dark side of man, which is human, but not preeminent or noble. Critics of capital punishment are quite correct in identifying its spirit and practice with those cultural dark ages in which people resolved their differences by violent force, in which superior force meant right, and in which human and animal violence was popular public entertainment. The degree to which such vengeful sentiments permeate American public opinion has already been alluded to. The implications of this will be examined more closely later.

If punishment is justifiable as a means of restoring justice and the moral order, it does not necessarily follow that capital punishment is just. First of all, there is the question of how well capital punishment may serve to restore justice and moral unity. Beyond that issue, there are other criteria to consider. The death penalty is not absolutely demanded by justice and social unity, even in grave crimes; some opponents would consider it excessive for these purposes. Neither justice nor unity is a simple matter of an eye-for-an-eye or a tooth-for-a-tooth; a principle of justice that grew out of vengeful motivations. The history of Western jurisprudence shows a steady progression away from tit for tat in punishment, especially in its corporal forms. We no longer tolerate the draconian barbarity of extorted confessions or punish criminals by maiming the offending physical organ. Punishments that arise out of a thirst for vengeance are inhumane, counterproductive, and unnecessary. Other stringent measures might serve as well to restore the order of justice and moral unity. Some proponents of capital punishment inconsistently argue that prolonged incarceration under life sentences is actually more punitive than the death penalty. A Gary Gilmore may prefer execution, a Charlie Brooks, Jr., may fight to the bitter end to live, even within grim prison walls. There are alternatives severe enough to be proportional, even to grave crimes. Life imprisonment or prolonged periods of incarceration, for 25 to 30 years, are indeed severe penalties.

Then, at worst, capital punishment "overcompensates" for the violation of justice and moral unity created by serious crimes. Under those circumstances, it is an unacceptable way to right the balance. In the last analysis, the legitimacy of capital punishment rests on other criteria. If those criteria commend it, the penalty of death may *also* serve to exact justice and affirm social trust. If they do not, other alternatives will suffice.

Capital Punishment and the Purposes of Punishment

In sum, only one among the various purposes of punishment appears to be arguable in the specific case of capital punishment. The death penalty serves no rehabilitative purpose; it exceeds the requirements of justice and social unity; alternatives to it may serve the same purpose as well; finally, the incapacitation or special deterrence of a given offender is insured by execution, but there are other effective ways to inhibit reoffending. In the latter two cases, the legitimacy of the death penalty rests on other criteria.

The general deterrence purpose is not so easy to evaluate. The protection of the innocent within the community is a compelling priority. Even the awful punishment of death might appear to be warranted if capital punishment were proven to be an effective marginal deterrent. It must be carefully determined whether or not capital punishment evidences such value. That alone is not enough, however. Whether or not the death penalty is a morally permissible punishment is also dependent on data relating to other effects of capital punishment. Social policies often achieve unintended results. There is no reason to presume that capital punishment is exceptional. These matters are considered in detail later in the book.

Moral Frameworks or Approaches

Arguments about capital punishment are related to its hypothetical purposes discussed above. They also reflect various approaches. Terminology and classifications vary, but for convenience, modes of argumentation will be categorized here as: (1) theological or scriptural; (2) humanitarian; and (3) for want of a better designation, operational or pragmatic. Each of these frames of reference requires brief comment.

The Scriptural Approach   Theological arguments pro and con the death penalty generally draw on scriptural authority. Citations of the Old and New Testaments can generate absolute judgments about the validity of capital punishment. In other words, proponents who employ scriptural texts infer that capital punishment is justified or even enjoined by the scriptures. Opponents who argue from the same base condemn the death penalty under all circumstances.

On the one hand, we are exhorted by the eye for an eye, tooth for a tooth, *quid pro quo* of the Old Testament. On the other, we are urged to adhere to the New Law admonitions to forgive and love our enemies, to turn the other cheek, and not to cast stones, or judge lest we be judged. Or we are urged to supersede justice with mercy. Some opponents of capital punishment also revert to the Old Testament and apply the fifth commandment to the state as well as to individual conduct.

It is difficult to emulate biblical example or to find justifications in the scripture when so many conflicting texts may be applied to the death penalty controversy. Moreover, literalism in this case is out of the mainstream of contemporary biblical criticism. In general, the Old Testament thrust is toward exact justice; the New Law superimposes charity and mercy. Nevertheless, Christian moralists have traditionally recognized the state's right to take life.

This right derived not only from the individual's right of self-defense, but from the right of the community to protect itself. Thus, when necessary, a law enforcement officer may employ deadly force, not only to protect himself, but to protect the community from serious harm. The state has been conceded the right to defend its citizens against others who would gravely injure them, by executing wrong-doers who are guilty of grave offenses. The state has no totalitarian authority, even *in extremis,* to protect the community at the expense of innocent individuals.

It should be emphasized that traditional Christian theology theoretically denies any absolute prohibition of the death penalty on scriptural authority. Moreover, it states a principal that requires application to specific circumstances, but does not itself assess those circumstances. At the risk of some oversimplification, the theological tradition appears to justify capital punishment primarily on the same deterrence grounds discussed earlier. It must be concluded that there is no validity in any absolute condemnation or endorsement of capital punishment on theological grounds. Rather, to paraphrase St. Paul, "by its fruits we shall know it." It is of far greater importance to assess the moral effects of capital punishment as it really works, rather than to attempt to interpret the scriptures.

The Humanitarian Approach   A second approach to the morality of capital punishment is the humanitarian frame of reference. Moral judgments about the death penalty are often overladen with senti-ment. Humanitarian ideas spring from ideals about human nature. However, they are heavily influenced by the feelings and attitudes that grow out of real experience with parents, peers, and others. It should be anticipated, for example, that law enforcers would lean in favor of capital punishment. It is not only their authority orien-tation which predisposes them to severe penalties, or that they are in a constant state of enmity with the criminal element. No doubt, their on-the-job experience, replete with the depradations and in-humane acts of offenders, inspires moral revulsion as well.

Favorability to the death penalty appears to be a highly emotion-laden reaction. Still, more often than not, it is the opponent of capital punishment who relies on the humanitarian or emotional argument. Some condemn the cold-blooded deliberations of the state, the ghoulish character of the rituals surrounding executions, and the sometimes elaborate lengths to which the state may go in insuring the life of the person prior to the date of the execution. This last irony is bitterly dismissed in the assertion that the state will spare no effort to insure that it is not deprived of its "pound of flesh." The agony of death row with its ominous uncertainty and sterility concern some. They allege that the psychic as well as physical pain of the capital punishment process are in themselves cruel and unusual (although there is little empirical research into the matter, and that which does exist offers little support to the contention.) Ironically, some of the eyewitnesses to the nation's first lethal injection execution by the state of Texas in December 1982 described the death of Charlie Brooks, Jr. as painful and protracted. What purported to be a more humane method of execution touched off a divisive debate within and without the medical profession about the ethical and humanitarian implications of lethal injection.

In the moral quotient, the proponents of capital punishment feel humanitarian concern for victims and their loved ones and to potential victims, including themselves. Opponents of the death penalty focus their humanitarian concerns on offenders. Abstractly, proponents interpret a society which is unduly permissive as dehumanizing, tolerant of even grave wrongdoing, and unwilling to invoke the death penalty in sufficient measure to affirm the sanctity of human life. A society in which the state itself takes life is characterized by opponents as brutalizing, setting a poor example for its citizenry in respect to the value of human life.

The debate about capital punishment can never be entirely liberated from emotions on either side of the issue. Still, it is necessary to try. It is historically evident that sound public policies are seldom if ever made in response to panic or the heightened emotions of the time. There are some very strongly *felt* reasons to support as well as to oppose the death penalty. Most opponents of capital punishment would be loathe to deny the compelling sufferings of victims and their survivors, if confronted by them. We are all frustrated and enraged by the tragic waste, senselessness, and cruelty of murder.

Most proponents of capital punishment support it from a distance. The data of carefully conducted research indicates that the proportion of supporters and the level of intensity of support varies considerably with the level of subjects' involvement with the death penalty. When proponents are placed in the position of hypothetically judging guilt or assigning penalties in capital trials, support for the death penalty erodes substantially. Most proponents of capital punishment would no doubt also be revolted if they were required to observe firsthand the ghoulish rituals surrounding execution and the event itself. Experienced prison officials such as Wardens Lewis Lawes and Clinton Duffy wrote eloquently of their opposition to the death penalty. Their position on the issue was heavily conditioned by the requirement of their official positions to participate in numerous executions. (See Duffy's *88 Men and 2 Women,* Doubleday, 1962, and Lawes's *Twenty Thousand Years in Sing Sing,* Long and Smith, 1932.)

Such sensibilities and the humanitarian impulses that engender them are eminently human and are, therefore, inevitable. They are not wrong in any moral sense, but they don't facilitate the resolution of basic issues involved. There are more compelling criteria on which to evaluate the death penalty. It is time to move on to those other considerations.

The Operational Approach   The third and final mode of moral argumentation about capital punishment is the operational or pragmatic mode. This approach focuses on how capital punishment is actually applied. What have been the consequences of the death penalty in the past and what might we expect them to be in the future? The operational approach is incompatible with any abstract prohibition or permission on the death penalty. It is evident from their separate written opinions that such pragmatic concerns were on the minds of the justices of the U.S. Supreme Court in the *Furman* case. It will be argued at various times in the progress of this book that most of the justices did not go far enough in addressing these realities, although for the first time they were directly confronted by the Court in *Furman.*

Pragmatic as it is, this approach rests firmly on principles of justice and is, therefore, a profoundly moral one. Justice is generally defined in terms of what one owes to others: i.e., justice involves interdependent rights and obligations. A commonly accepted synonym for justice is fairness. Three kinds of justice have been distinguished in ethics and jurisprudence. Commutative justice involves what one individual or party owes to another. Failures to fulfill contractual obligations are violations of commutative justice. Social justice encompasses the obligations of individuals or groups to the greater community. An employer who amasses profits at the expense of a living wage for the workers provides a classic example of the violation of social justice. A more current example is the chemical company that deliberately or negligently pollutes the environment. Finally, distributive justice directs the state in its distribution of benefits and burdens to the citizenry. Distributive justice is concerned, for example, with the obligation of the state to apportion taxes in accord with individual abilities to pay, or with the obligation of the community to create conditions of life which permit all citizens to realize their human potential.

Proponents of capital punishment often reflect a general public confusion about the purposes of the criminal justice system. They mistakenly cast that system in the role of guardian of commutative justice; they assign responsibility to the police, courts, and corrections to insure that individual rights are safeguarded and that "justice" is provided for the murdered victim or for his loved ones. In reality, the civil court is the institution that societies have created to oversee commutative justice. The criminal justice system deals with social and distributive justice. It is concerned primarily with the interdependent rights and obligations of the individual and society.

This confusion about purposes of the criminal justice system is of great importance. It leads to the misidentification of the system as an agency of personal retribution. It fosters a negativism, even a hostility toward offenders on the part of officials in the system which affects their day-to-day operations. On the other hand, arguments which oppose capital punishment on operational grounds are concerned precisely with the role of the criminal justice system in effecting social and distributive justice.

Such arguments raise serious questions about the disprivileged economic and cultural backgrounds which characterize the overwhelming number of offenders who have been executed. They also raise serious questions about the way in which the criminal justice system functions, and the way that it ought to function, the miscarriage of justice, and the execution of the innocent. It questions disparities in power and resources and resultant inequalities before the law. It questions discrimination in the application of the death penalty on racial or socioeconomic grounds. And it questions theoretical deficiencies that are inherent in the criminal justice system itself.

Summary

Capital punishment is not rehabilitative, nor is it needed to incapacitate the offender, to restore the order of justice, or to reinforce social unity. The only general purpose of punishment that *may* be better served by the death penalty than by some alternative is that of marginal deterrence. The purposes of punishment are not, however, the only criteria for judging its morality. Absolute theological and humanitarian arguments against the death penalty were found to be equivocal and inconclusive. Instead, it was proposed that capital punishment is immoral on pragmatic or operational grounds: it has always been unjustly applied and, given the realities of human society, it can hardly be otherwise. This conclusion rests on evidence and a chain of linking generalizations that will now be presented in a fuller, systematic way.

QUESTIONS FOR REFLECTION AND DISCUSSION

1.   Is there a hierarchy among the purposes of punishment? If so, what is the principle of priority?

2.   In this chapter, the desire for justice is distinguished from the desire for retribution. Consider the attitudes of persons whom you know. How does their perception of this purpose relate to their attitude toward capital punishment?

3.   List the various scriptural references to capital punishment that you have heard, read, or identified on your own. Discuss their pros and cons.

4.   Consider possible ways to prioritize humanitarian arguments for and against the death penalty.

5.   Consider the various indicators that the criminal law addresses the interests of the community. Relate your discussion to the purposes of punishment.

6.   Are there human behaviors which can be morally evaluated by the direct application of absolute principles? Can principles be applied to circumstances?

MISCARRIAGE OF JUSTICE

There are two distinct ways in which justice may miscarry. In an absolute sense, an individual may be erroneously convicted and suffer punishment for something he did not do. Ordinarily this is what is meant when we speak of a miscarriage of justice. There is another way that injustice occurs. While guilty, one individual may be punished with greater severity than another who is equally guilty of the same offense. It is unfair to punish an individual who is innocent of wrongdoing, or to impose a more severe penalty on one person than on another for the same crime when they are equally culpable.

Miscarriage of Justice

Let us first consider the case of wrong conviction and punishment. We are all too often forced to concede the imperfection of the human administration of justice. While not commonplace, erroneous convictions for serious felonies, including aggravated murder, are not rare either. The celebrated case of the Delaware priest who was accused of a string of notorious armed robberies is well known. The

31

subsequent plausible confession to the crimes by another individual not even suspected in the case illustrates the fallibility of even "certain" and numerous eyewitness identifications. Lenell Geter's case also illustrates the point. Geter, a young black, spent sixteen months in a Texas prison on armed robbery charges. He would almost certainly still be languishing there if a CBS "60 Minutes" program had not exposed the injustices created by the gross malfunctions of the criminal justice system.

The same kind of defects can operate in death penalty cases as well. Capital crimes are heinous crimes that arouse strong emotions in the community. In the instance of aggravated murder there are unusual pressures to make arrests and to punish the wrongdoers. Constitutional safeguards such as the guarantee of an unbiased jury, or the right to a change of venue, or relocation of the trial have restricted applications. As celebrated cases like the Dreyfus Affair or even the Rosenbergs' case suggest, we ought to be especially wary of the justice process when, for one reason or another, the crime or the accused arouses strong antipathies.

Appellate Review and Miscarriage

Despite often lengthy appellate review in capital cases, there is no way to be certain about the accuracy or truth of the evidence produced at trial. Appeals courts do not retry criminal cases on the issue of guilt or innocence, and only rarely do they review the technical issue of the sufficiency of the evidence. In 1982, the U.S. Supreme Court appeared to dilute the concept of the sufficiency of the evidence itself when it permitted Florida to retry Delbert Tibbs. Tibbs had originally been convicted of the rape of a young woman and the murder of her companion. In 1976 the Florida Supreme Court had set aside Tibbs's conviction on the grounds of insufficient evidence. In 1981, with two new justices sitting, that court overruled itself and required Tibbs to stand retrial. On appeal, the U.S. Supreme Court voted five to four against Tibbs's arguments of harassment and double jeopardy and permitted him to be retried. In the opinion of the court, Justice O'Connor distinguished between the "sufficiency" of the evidence and the "weight" of the evidence. The former refers to the minimal amount of evidence necessary to support a guilty verdict; the latter to the reweighing of the evidence by the appellate court, a role reserved to the jury.

If Jim Mann is correct in his assessment of the import of the Charlie Brooks, Jr. case, even the careful judicial review process in capital cases will be short-cut in the future. Writing in a syndicated *Los Angeles Times* article shortly after Brooks's execution, Mann suggested that "by refusing to block Brooks's execution, the Supreme Court gave its sanction to a new short-cut procedure for handling death penalty appeals." Historically, death penalty appeals for state convicts have been three-tiered: (1) appeals (generally automatic) through the state courts with eventual appeals to the U.S. Supreme Court; (2) if unsuccessful, a *habeas corpus* action in the state trial court, which may test the legality of the appellant's detention on procedural grounds (rather than his guilt or innocence), appeals through the state courts, and a second hearing by the U.S. Supreme Court; and (3) if still unsuccessful, another *habeas corpus* action, brought this time in the U.S. District Court, with subsequent appeals to the U.S. Court of Appeals, and ultimately once again to the U.S. Supreme Court. Brooks availed himself of the first two tiers without success. When he attempted to bring his case to the federal courts directly, the District Court declined to hear the merits of his case or to stay his execution. Both the U.S. Court of Appeals and the U.S. Supreme Court refused to stay the execution or hear the merits of the case. In effect, the federal courts refused to hear (for the third time) Brooks's appeal on his conviction and sentence.

Some forthright proponents of capital punishment such as Supreme Court Justice William Rehnquist have argued that the appellate process has been unduly protracted and no doubt would rejoice if curtailed in the future. Will it be? Is the Brooks case a harbinger? There are increasing indications that it is. In the spring of 1983, the Supreme Court decided a case that is widely regarded as further limiting the ability to appeal in death penalty cases. Meanwhile, Justice Lewis Powell, in a speech to a judicial conference on May 9, 1983, called for the courts to expedite death penalty cases. A proponent of the death penalty, Powell urged that unless the execution process can be speeded up, state legislatures should abolish capital punishment. These are disquieting signs.

The Brooks case is especially well suited for examination in this context. The state never established whether it was Charlie Brooks, Jr. or his accomplice who actually pulled the trigger in the kidnap-murder for which they were separately tried. And Brooks and his accomplice weren't telling. At the same time, the U.S. Supreme Court ruled in the summer of 1982 that the death penalty was excessive, cruel and unusual and, therefore, unconstitutional when imposed on an accomplice who did not directly participate in a felony murder. Charlie Brooks, Jr. may have been guilty of many things, including kidnapping. He might even have pulled that trigger and been guilty of aggravated murder. Then again, he might not have been; apparently the state did not prove beyond a reasonable doubt that he fired the fatal shot. On a purely statistical basis (all hunches aside), there was only a fifty-fifty chance that Charlie Brooks, Jr., fired the shot. His execution may be fairly judged as unconstitutional, even though, ironically, the Supreme Court refused to apply its own recently derived principle to the case.

Data on Miscarriage in Capital Cases

Several studies have verified substantial levels of erroneous convictions for first degree murders. Among them is the historical research of Hugo Bedau, one of the most astute students of capital punishment in the United States. Bedau's survey of the years 1893 to 1962 produced 74 cases in which "wrongful conviction of criminal homicide was alleged and in most cases proven beyond a doubt." In 40 of these cases, individuals had received life sentences or less, in three cases conviction had been "averted," and in 31, the death penalty was imposed. Eight of these persons had unfortunately been executed. Professor Bedau expresses his incredulity that in only a small percentage of these cases did judicial review discover and rectify the miscarriage.

In 1971, Bedau augmented his 1962 survey by reporting on "a far from complete listing" of additional wrong convictions for homicide since 1962. He identifies three cases in New York and one each in South Carolina, Florida, Pennsylvania, and Texas. A few other studies, even more current than Bedau's, have also produced evidence relevant to the question of miscarriages in first degree homicide cases.

Numbers are of secondary importance, in any event. The death penalty is a terrible one, and it is horrible to contemplate the execution of innocent persons in the past or future. Moreover, the death penalty is irrevocable; there is no redress for miscarriage of justice.

Legal Theory and Miscarriages

The execution of an innocent person, even unintentionally, is an affront to the principles of Anglo-American jurisprudence. In this system the burden of proof beyond a reasonable doubt is placed squarely on the state. The safeguards gradually extended to the accused under the Fourth, Fifth, Sixth, Eighth, and Fourteenth Amendments to the U.S. Constitution are directed toward the state proving its case. Today it is recognized as elemental fair play that an accusation is not tantamount to a conclusion of guilt, and that the state must establish that guilt. The accused may or may not choose to confront his accuser in his own defense, but he is not convicted except on evidence against him produced by the government.

The state's obligation to prove guilt and the requirement of fair procedures in doing so are based on particularly cherished values. First, there is the recognition of the worth of the human individual and of his vulnerability in the face of the superior power and resources of the state. Second, underlying the Anglo-American law is the conviction that it is better that some who are guilty go free than that one innocent person be punished unjustly.

Irrevocability of Capital Punishment

As a practical matter, the occurrence of inadvertent errors cannot be permitted to emasculate the criminal justice system. The community must certainly be permitted to protect itself, even at the risk of error. However, the state is able to make recompense when it errs. If the state is just and humane, it acknowledges its error and its responsibility to ungrudgingly rectify it. Capital punishment is a distinct case. The punishment is horrendous and nothing is salvageable—there is not even minimal redress for mistakes when miscarriage of justice is aggravated by the punishment of death. It is irresponsible and immoral to shrug our shoulders and dismiss the execution of the innocent as a tragic but unavoidable by-product or necessity. It is unfortunate but understandable when a police officer mistakenly takes innocent life in the heat and confusion of a threatening moment. The state hardly has the same justification; it acts with cold-blooded deliberation and detachment.

What is so nonsensical and so awful about the willingness to gamble on the guilt or innocence of every subject for execution is that capital punishment serves no demonstrable utilitarian purpose. Were there substantial reason to believe that it deterred, then the sacrifice of a few innocent lives might at least be understandable, if unacceptable. As shall be discussed later in detail, the overwhelming weight of research affords no evidence of deterrence. Neither justice nor community solidarity justify such a sacrifice. The need to fit the punishment to the crime can be satisfied short of a life for a life. A major concern of most of those who oppose the death penalty is well summarized in a remark variously attributed to Thomas Jefferson or the Marquis de LaFayette. Its origin is perhaps of lesser import than its substance: "I shall ask for the abolition of the punishment of death until I shall have the infallibility of human justice demonstrated to me."

Disparities in Punishment

Another way in which injustice may result from the administration of justice is when any two individuals who commit equally serious crimes are punished unequally. The more systematic kinds of group inequalities, those resulting from racial discrimination, economic limitations, etc., are the subject of the next chapter. For now, let us turn to those situations in which the everyday operations of the criminal justice system itself create disparities in punishments.

An illustration may be helpful. During the second World War in the European theater of operations, one of the most tragically curious events in the modern history of the American military occurred. Private Eddie Slovik became the first (and only) American soldier to be executed for desertion in the face of the enemy since the Civil War. William Bradford Huie, the renowned investigative journalist, wrote an early chronicle of the incident in a book entitled, *The Execution of Private Slovik*. Many years later, Slovik's ill and aging widow instituted suit against an implacable government, seeking payment of the military insurance benefits denied her on the basis of Slovik's dishonorable death. Around the same time, one of the national television networks also presented the Slovik story in a docudrama.

Unfortunately, Mrs. Slovik and Huie offered little understanding of the execution of Slovik. Slovik's fears and behavior are understandable enough. A loser, a slum kid who had done time in

Michigan's Ionia Reformatory for petty property crimes, Eddie Slovik was hardly an All-American boy. In his foreword to the Huie book, General Lewis B. Hershey, for many years the director of Selective Service, condemned the combat replacement system, used in Slovik's time. Hershey noted that the individual movement of replacement troops into on-line combat units was no longer employed in the American Army. Eddie Slovik, a green soldier without previous combat experience, was moved forward and ordered to join his new unit in the middle of an enemy artillery fusillade. He panicked and deserted.

What is more difficult to comprehend is the reason for the execution. Convicted by court martial and sentenced to death, Slovik's case made its way through the military appeals process. Ultimately a preoccupied General Eisenhower, Supreme Allied Commander, signed the execution order and Eddie Slovik died. He might well have asked, "Why me, oh Lord?" Slovik reputedly maintained that he was being executed for stealing a few loaves of bread when he was a hungry kid. Some attributed the execution to the typical bureaucratic snafu characteristic of military organizations. In any event, the execution of Eddie Slovik was an exceptional occurrence. He was only one of many World War II soldiers who deserted in combat or otherwise failed to perform their duties. There were deserters in wars before and after. His execution was eccentric, irrational, and meaningless from any point of view.

Discretion and Punishment

The pathetic case of Eddie Slovik suggests to us the defectiveness of human justice. The criminal law permits officials at every level of the justice system to exercise broad discretion. The police officer's discretion is centered in his power of arrest, but it may also be exercised in other areas as well. For example, the police make an initial determination on prosecution by selecting those cases which will go to the prosecutor for his action. Police behavior with regard to search and seizure, custodial interrogation, and other processes involve exercises of power that can affect the successful prosecution in cases.

The judge also has great discretion within the limits of the statutes. In ruling on motions, charging the jury, etc., judges exercise great power. While such judicial exercises of authority are subject to review in the appellate courts, broad discretionary power in sentencing remains intact in most states today, in spite of the movement toward mandatory sentences (automatic incarceration with no probation option) and toward sentences for fixed terms (determinate sentences).

Police discretion is considerably less of a problem in capital cases, since the gravity of the offenses involved requires that all such cases be referred for prosecution. This is not to suggest that the bias or unprofessional conduct on the part of law enforcement officers cannot affect the outcome of cases. As Kenneth Gross alleges in *The Alice Crimmins Case,* the police always have the ability to enhance the strength of a case or to ignore evidence favorable to the defense, even in murder cases. Alice Crimmins was the principal in a notorious homicide case in the early 1970s. She was a young, attractive divorcee, living with her small daughter and son in a Queens, New York apartment. In spite of her own consistent protestations of innocence, Mrs. Crimmins was indicted and convicted for the grisly murders of her children. Gross and others have presented a strong case for the possibility that certain police officers assigned to the investigation prejudged Alice Crimmins. Apparently, Mrs. Crimmins's swinging lifestyle and her seeming disregard for the day-to-day care of her children offended and antagonized certain key investigators. Critics of the investigation suggest that the fundamental moral stances of these investigators inclined them to stereotype Alice Crimmins as an unfit, unloving mother who regarded her children as nuisances, getting in the way of her pleasure. They argue that these officers shaped the evidence in such a way as to incriminate Alice Crimmins.

In most cases, the choices of when to arrest or to decline to arrest for murder, or to refer for prosecution or not are practically limited by the gravity of the offense. Likewise the discretion of the judge or the jury (when the jury imposes sentence) have been circumscribed in the sequel to the Supreme Court capital punishment decisions of the 1970s. When the Supreme Court struck down "jury discretionary" statutes in *Furman,* and subsequently approved "guided discretionary statutes" in *Gregg,* it in effect required that the legislature assume greater control over sentencing in capital cases. The Court's intention in limiting discretion was to eliminate disparities in sentences by restricting the choices permitted to sentencing authorities. Objective sentences could be compelled by writing aggravating and mitigating factors into the law. The result should be equality in punishment. Such has not, however, been entirely the result. Let us examine why.

In the first instance, there is no effective way to retain any semblance of choice and yet entirely eliminate arbitrary decisions. The provision of aggravating and mitigating circumstances ensures a more objective formula for judgment, but there is no guarantee that judges or jurors will use it. There is still room for personal biases to operate, both in the guilt determination phase and in the process of weighing the evidence on mitigation and aggravation themselves. There is, of course, no way to entirely inhibit the intrusion of bias into the determination of verdicts. The only ironclad method of insuring equality at the sentencing stage would be the mandatory death penalty for all capital offenders, a solution which the Supreme Court denied in *Woodson* v. *North Carolina* and similar cases.

Unique Powers of Prosecutors

While the Supreme Court placed limits on the discretion of the sentencers, that of prosecutors remains largely unfettered. In some respects, the role of the prosecutor is the most powerful in the criminal justice system. To begin with, he is at the heart of the process, midway between law enforcement and the courts. The courts are largely reactive because the initiative remains with the prosecutor. As long as the prosecutor retains favorable public opinion, his discretion is very broad indeed, and he has much influence over selective law enforcement policies. He is the community's chief law enforcer and how prostitution, gambling, pornography, and other statutory offense categories are handled is singularly influenced by him. Of course, initiative on such matters also rests with law enforcement decision makers, but wise police executives take their cues from the prosecutor. Failure to do so would be at best unproductive, and at worst, self-defeating.

The prosecutor also has the power to initiate proceedings in the individual's case because he controls the accusation process. Theoretically, of course, the prosecutor is limited by the law and by the evidence available to him. In practice, he has a lot of room in which to maneuver. Either he files accusations directly by the process of information, or brings them to the grand jury. But he controls the grand jury by determining what evidence grand jurors will hear. Since grand jury hearings are closed, and non-adversarial by definition, there is no opposition to the prosecutor, either by defense cross-examination or by a defense case presented in its own right. Not all states require indictment by grand jury; some permit prosecutors to file charges directly with the courts through a process known as accusation by information. In neither case is the process very protective of the rights or the reputation of the accused.

The Central Role of Plea Bargaining   Perhaps the most important power held by prosecutors is that directly related to plea bargaining. Within statutory limits they have wide discretion in charging offenders because they determine what violations to levy against the individual, how many counts on each violation, penalties to be sought after, and whether or not leniency will be recommended.

Whether the stimulus to negotiate originates with defense counsel or with the prosecutor, the basis for negotiation is always with the prosecutor because the charging function is his. It is estimated that an astounding 90 percent of all criminal cases are disposed of nationally by guilty pleas, most of them negotiated. It is clearly evident, therefore, that the prosecutor's initiative in bringing charges against the individual, and his options in doing so, is the very dynamic that make the system go. Law enforcers and the courts are indispensable, but they are not as pivotal in the system.

Prosecutors acquiesce in plea bargaining for many reasons. In some cases, a reduction in charges is commended by saving time, money, and prosecutorial and judicial resources. Chief Justice Warren Burger has frequently reiterated his concern about logjams in the trial and appellate courts. Burger has calculated that if the proportion of all cases presently tried were increased from 10 percent to only 20 percent, twice as many courtrooms, judges, bailiffs, prosecutors, etc. would be required to handle the increase.

In some cases, plea bargains satisfy the needs of not only prosecutors, but other major role players in the system as well. The prosecutor augments his conviction record, the judge decreases his overcrowded docket, and defense counsel gets a substantial retainer without the need of detailed preparation and trial. Some critics of the plea bargaining syndrome are especially sensitive to abuse in this regard. They see the potential for self-interest to foster symbiotic relationships between supposed adversaries. It is possible that the interests of the defendant, or of the community, may become secondary to those of the prosecutor and defense counsel. Judicial indifference or even complicity may also be encouraged in the same way.

Sometimes prosecutors are especially willing to bargain when their case is weak or when they calculate that the evidence may not be strong enough to sustain a charge of greater gravity. The prosecutor may be aware of technical deficiencies in police or pretrial procedures. He might, therefore, deem it questionable whether or not a conviction could be sustained on appeal. For all such reasons, the prosecutor may rationalize that it is preferable to remove the individual from the streets, albeit for a shorter time, than to risk losing him on a more serious charge.

Plea Bargaining and Unequal Punishments   For whatever reasons the prosecutor charges or bargains as he does, prosecutorial discretion may and often does lead to inequalities in punishment. Obviously, the disposition in any two similar cases may vary in relationship to such factors as the degree of connectedness of defense counsel, their bargaining skills and those of the prosecutor, the prosecutor's perception of the strength of his case, the exigencies or even the whims of the moment. Such factors have little to do, of course, with the degree of culpability of the offenders themselves. Often, they have nothing to do with the degree of danger that the offenders pose to society. One of the highly questionable outcomes of plea bargaining is exemplified by the fact that sentences meted out on conviction subsequent to trial are on the whole more punitive than those imposed in response to guilty pleas. Incidentally, the U.S. Supreme Court has yet to review these research findings. Many others are uneasy about an apparent penalty rebounding on those who have the temerity to insist upon invoking their rights under the Fifth Amendment not to incriminate themselves and their Sixth Amendment rights to a speedy and public trial. They would insist that plea bargaining runs counter to American legal principles, which uphold the innocence of the accused until proven guilty, and the *state's* obligation to establish guilt beyond a reasonable doubt.

The Prosecutor, Plea Bargaining, and Discretion in the Imposition of the Death Penalty

These day-to-day operations of the criminal justice system take on ghastly proportions when considered in the case of capital punishment. The *Furman* and *Gregg* cases purported to limit discretion at only one level of the system. While judges and juries must refer to statutory guidelines and while the death sentences they suggest are often subjected to review by the state's highest court, no constitutional rule has yet been invoked to limit the discretion of prosecutors in capital cases. On the contrary, the Supreme Court has been reluctant to restrict such discretion at all. In the *Gregg* case, the Court explicitly limited the requirement of structured discretion to the judicial process. Neither the exercise of discretion by the prosecutor before trial nor that of the governor in exercising executive clemency after conviction and sentencing are covered by *Furman* and *Gregg*. Furthermore, the Court has put its imprimatur on the pragmatic practice of plea bargaining, consistently upholding it and the sentencing disparities which it creates. The justification of the Court is perhaps best summarized in a 1970 case, *Brady* v. *United States*. Mr. Justice White's opinion for the Court in that case offers an interesting rationalization, part of which is quoted below:

> But we cannot hold that it is unconstitutional for the state to extend a benefit to a defendant who in turn extends a substantial benefit to the State and who demonstrates by his plea that he is ready and willing to admit his crime and to enter the correctional system in a frame of mind that affords hope for success in rehabilitation over a shorter period of time than might otherwise be necessary.

Justice White's argument not only makes a virtue out of expediency; it is naive, if not downright cavalier to emphasize the rehabilitative benefits of plea bargaining. It may well be of rehabitative advantage to spend as little time as one can in America's prisons, since their track records are so very poor on that score. Nevertheless, dissatisfaction and cynicism with sentencing disparities as well as with parole decisions are generally recognized as major causes of inmate unrest. In fact, much of the impetus toward determinate or fixed sentencing comes from opposition to such disparities.

Knowing that this is the way in which the system routinely operates, we ought to have additional serious reservations about the death penalty. Again, it is impossible to eliminate every vestige of choice from human endeavors. We do what we can to guide choices into channels that are consistent with our fundamental social values, and we live with whatever imperfection remains. The death penalty is, however, a different matter. It is an enormous, qualitatively different penalty which must be distinguished in all respects from all other punishments.

The conscience of the community ought to agonize over the execution of Charlie Brooks, Jr. His accomplice might have been the murderer, and he won a technical reversal of his original conviction, and the prosecutor's decision subsequently to bargain rather than retry his case netted him a 40-year sentence. Under Texas law, he will be eligible for parole in six and a half years. Meanwhile Charlie Brooks, Jr., is dead. The vindictive would lament only that Brooks's accomplice was not also executed and would curse the courts for overprotecting the guilty. The moral lesson of the Brooks case would entirely escape their notice. The lesson is clear: it is unjust and immoral to execute one individual for a crime equal in gravity and guilt to that of another who suffers a lesser penalty. Especially when human life hangs in the balance, there can be no justice by lottery, by caprice, or out of expedience.

Judicial Review and Failures in Discretion

During the 1983–84 term, the U.S. Supreme Court planned to clarify the issue of the proportional application of the death penalty. The thrust of *Furman, Gregg,* and related cases has been to require the state to apply the death penalty evenly to cases of similar kind (i.e., relative to aggravating and mitigating factors). Indeed, state courts of last resort appeared to have been compelled to insure that individual cases in which the death penalty is imposed are comparable to other cases in which the death penalty has been utilized.

Justice Stewart's opinion in *Gregg* appeared to endorse the principle of proportionality review as a safeguard against arbitrary and capricious imposition of the death penalty. Thus in reviewing the protracted procedures required by law for review of death sentences by the Georgia Supreme Court, he writes: "If the Court affirms a death sentence, it is required to include in its decision *reference to similar cases that it has taken into consideration*" (emphasis added). And in the *Woodson* case, he noted that the absence of such review procedures was a deficiency in the mandatory death penalty statute enacted by North Carolina. Still, in January of 1984 the Court ruled in the Harris case that such a review was not constitutionally required of California and other states.

It would seem that the most effective way to try to insure that capital punishment is not being imposed arbitrarily or capriciously (or discriminatorily, if one concedes the possibility of discrimination) would be through the imposition of some norm such as that afforded by proportionality review. The defect in this approach is obvious. There is no requirement that death penalty cases be compared with other murder cases in which the death penalty *is not* imposed. The point is illustrated by a Butler County, Ohio, case disposed of on December 2, 1983. A 22-year-old man charged with aggravated murder, kidnapping, and aggravated robbery in the murder of a 78-year-old stroke victim, pleaded guilty to the charges and was sentenced to life imprisonment in one day (*Cincinnati Post,* December 3, 1983). Meanwhile, neighboring Hamilton County (Cincinnati's home county) has often been criticized for overapplication of the death penalty.

The role of negotiations in the Butler County defendant's plea of guilty to a heinous crime obviates the impact of prosecutorial discretion on the application of capital punishment. Prosecutorial discretion renders nonsensical the notion that the death penalty can be imposed fairly and evenly.

Miscarriages, Inequities, and the Dignity of the Person

A society must always be vigilant against becoming hardened and cynical. Mass society predisposes us to think of personal tragedy with detachment, to measure the cost of human life in numbers. The destruction and slaughter of three modern wars, the potential for nuclear holocaust, exposure to world starvation and malnutrition, murder and mayhem in our midst, the cynical exploitation of violent themes by the media condition us to be indifferent to the tragedy of ending a single human life. It is all too easy to dismiss the execution of the innocent as a rarity. It is tempting to rationalize that if one dies and another is only incarcerated for the same crime, the executed person was guilty anyway. It sounds plausible when we hear that too much should not be made of the imperfections of the justice system because the protection of the community is at stake. The community is, however, composed of individual persons. What diminishes one of us diminishes us all.

QUESTIONS FOR REFLECTION AND DISCUSSION

1. What should be the state's obligations when justice miscarries?

2. Weigh the factors that protect against or conversely enhance the possibility of miscarriage of justice in capital cases.

3. What are the implications of the discretion exercised by criminal justice functionaries?

4. Discuss how individualizing justice and rehabilitation conflicts with equitable sentencing.

5. A few jurisdictions have apparently limited plea bargaining substantially. Otherwise, how might the practice be made more effective?

6. Consider that poor people have higher infant and adult mortality and morbidity rates, lower life expectations, etc. Would you anticipate that their limited resources would seriously disadvantage them in the justice system?

_____

Chapter Four

DISCRIMINATION AND CAPITAL PUNISHMENT

Nowhere in American society are racial and socioeconomic divisions more apparent than in the criminal justice system. The typical criminal defendant is a lower class male, young, indigent, usually black. He is less educated than the general population, his employment history is less stable, and frequently he has problems with alcohol or drug abuse, mental illness or deficiency, etc. He is almost always represented by a public defender, or occasionally in rural areas, by a court-appointed attorney. The criminal court dockets in state jurisdictions contain few white-collar crime prosecutions. White-collar offenders are more often prosecuted in the federal district courts, when prosecuted at all. The same generalizations can be applied to members of organized crime, who are also under-represented in the justice system clientele. The pronounced over-representation of lower class and minority people progresses through various levels of the justice system, from arrest through incarceration. It is generally recognized among criminologists that poor and minority persons are prone to arrest, conviction, and incarceration.

The unintended effect of the criminal law is to create a virtual state of opposition between the largely white middle and upper

46

classes and the minority untouchables of American society. Law enforcement, court and corrections systems are financed primarily by middle- and upper-class taxpayers. Their purpose is to sustain and protect many values and interests that have lesser significance to lower class people. From the lower class perspective, the criminal justice functionary—the police officer, judge, or corrections officer—is frequently seen as the enemy. In a class conscious way, lower-class people often perceive the justice system as an instrument of repression by society.

Vulnerability of Lower Classes

Lower-class people and those on the economic margin have little impact on the formulation of criminal laws or the administration of criminal justice, although they are more vulnerable to it. Unlike the white-collar or organized criminal, they lack resources, power, and connections which might protect them against law enforcers or assist them in defending themselves in court. Their neighborhoods are high-crime-rate areas and their behavior is much more carefully scrutinized. A ghetto youngster's petty theft is, therefore, much more severely treated than the behavior of the young suburban vandal who does wheelies on household lawns or mows down rows of mailboxes. The poor lack alternative resources. For them there are no private psychiatric clinics, no expensive military academies, or other private boarding schools for their children. There are, instead, the juvenile court, the detention facility, or the state training school.

Poor people are less able to make restitution for property crimes involving any more than minor amounts and the courts are not very willing to allow them to try. The poor cannot resolve their criminal difficulties by simply resigning their positions or repaying their victims. Well-heeled white-collar offenders can embezzle or steal hundreds of thousands of dollars and never do jail time. Frequently they are permitted to resign their positions on private agreements to make restitution. If prosecuted and convicted, they are fined, ordered to make restitution, and placed on probation. Again and again we hear the most hard-bitten law-and-order judges rationalize such sentences on the grounds that these offenders have been punished enough by public exposure and loss of reputation and job. All the petty property criminal has to lose is his liberty, fresh air, and sunlight.

Minority persons and poor whites lack status in the community. They are not "respectable" people. Thus, they elicit no sympathy in the criminal justice system. Instead they are collectively society's burden. They lack poise, a positive demeanor, and they are inarticulate. No amount of temporary grooming and coaching at the hands of defense counsel can alter the stigma of the streets.

Lower class people have considerably less going for them in the community such as jobs, strong familial bonds, or organizational affiliations. Consequently they are less suitable candidates for release on recognizance bonds, probation, or other alternatives to incarceration, unless institutions are already bursting at the seams or correctional budgets are already bulging. The police and courts have become exasperated by large numbers of lower-class petty offenders and their failure to deter them.

At every stage of the criminal justice process, the proportion of those who are forced through the system is increasingly lower-class and black. In some states about half of the population in institutions for felons is black. Criminologists have long been in general agreement that the disproportionately high percentage of lower-class people in official crime statistics is caused by disparities in the operation of the criminal justice system. It is only the extent to which such disparities account for the disproportion observed that is debatable. Differences in life conditions and in lifestyles—economic impoverishment and the culture that it produces—are also no doubt instrumental.

Legal Defense of the Poor

A particularly critical dimension is that of the lesser ability of the typical defendant to defend himself against the judicial process. It has taken us a long time to recognize certain truths implicit in our theory of justice. The essential presumption of the adversary process is that, if the prosecution puts on its best case, and if the defense counters with the best it has to offer, truth will be produced by the conflict. The inevitability of such an outcome might be somewhat dubious, but in theory this process appears to be superior to alternative possibilities.

The law itself, legal procedures, and evidence-gathering techniques have become increasingly more sophisticated. The Sixth Amendment right of an accused to have specialized assistance in his own defense has, therefore, taken on increasingly greater meaning. The U.S. Supreme Court has gradually recognized the need in adversarial proceedings to balance the defendant's side of the equation. In a series of right-to-counsel cases landmarked by *Powell* v. *Alabama* (1932), *Gideon* v. *Wainwright* (1963) and *Argersinger* v. *Hamlin* (1972), the Court extended the right of counsel to indigent defendants in state trials. The *Powell* case granted counsel to the indigent in capital cases, *Gideon* in all felony cases and ultimately, *Argersinger* extended the right in all cases where the loss of liberty was possible, even on misdemeanor charges.

While such attempts to vitalize the Sixth Amendment are commendable, they could not in themselves entirely assure equality before the law. It is not enough to simply change the law; it is also necessary to change the institutional pattern of the delivery of legal services. The growth of public advocacy agencies in criminal cases represents such an institutional adaptation to the spirit of *Gideon* and *Argersinger*. While it repudiates the inadequate court appointment approach which preceded it, the public defender office still leaves much to be desired.

There are many dedicated, highly competent public defenders who are admirable individual practitioners. At the same time, the poor funding in public defender agencies creates bottom-heaviness in staffing. Younger, less experienced attorneys tend to be more numerous than in private criminal law firms which specialize in the trial of criminal cases. Even more restrictive are budgetary limits on staff size and the inadequacies of case preparation which arise from far too many cases with far too few attorneys to handle them.

Data provided by the National Legal Aid and Defender Association shed considerable light on the matter. A 1973 survey identified 650 defender systems serving indigent defendants in 28 percent of the counties of the United States. The Association enumerated about 2,600 full-time public defenders nationally. Meanwhile the Association estimated that there are almost four million arrests annually for felonies, non-traffic misdemeanors, and juvenile offenses in which individuals are financially unable to retain their own lawyers. The Association realistically projected that if 25 percent of these four million defendants were represented by court appointments from the private bar, 14,000 additional public defenders would be neeeded to adequately defend the remainder. The simple fact is that as late as 1973, public defender agencies had less than one-fifth of the professional manpower that the Legal Aid and Defender Association judged necessary to do a good job. Given steady increases in the general population and the crime rate, it is unlikely that staffing ratios in public defender agencies have improved all that much over the last decade. Indeed, given economic conditions and the cuts in public budgets of recent years, there may have been some losses in that area.

These data make it abundantly clear that the spirit of constitutional rulings has not been very well matched by institutional provisions for representation of the indigent defendant. Prosecutors would no doubt quickly respond that they too could use additional funds for more attorneys, paralegals, investigators, and staff support. They would no doubt point out that as public agencies they also operate under fiscal restraints. They do, but it must be remembered that prosecutors are assisted in their preparation of cases by the evidence gathered by police. Moreover, the prosecuting attorney is a traditional, well-established agent of the American criminal justice. And the prosecutor's office ranks considerably higher in the public's hierarchy of priorities than the public defender's office. The public views the function of the prosecutor as protective of its interests and well-being. There is little general public concern about serving the legal needs of those who are accused of violating the public good by committing crimes. This is particularly evident in the present period of fear and outrage about crime and the negative climate regarding civil liberties.

It must also be kept in mind that competent representation by counsel is not the only prerequisite for successful defense against criminal accusation. Witnesses may leave jurisdictions between indictment and trial and someone must pay the cost of their return to testify. Expert witnesses (psychiatrists, pathologists, etc.) are frequently as invaluable to the defense as to the prosecutor, and their services can be very expensive. Investigative resources can be highly effective in unearthing new evidence, tracing witnesses, etc. Many of these services are routinely available to the prosecution and more can always be provided if they are essential to the prosecutor's case. Few of them are available in the run-of-the-mill defense case. A few jurisdictions, including the federal, make paltry sums available, usually under the control of the trial judge, to assist in providing such "auxilliary" services to the defendant.

The financial resources of the state are superior to those of the defendant. As noted earlier, this collective advantage is implicitly recognized in Anglo-American jurisprudence. The Bill of Rights was intended to prevent tyranny originating in any branch of government. No system of safeguards is fail-safe, however, and the fewer the resources of the individual, the more vulnerable he is to the superior power of the state.

Variations in the Quality of Defense   There is an additional dimension to the matter of counsel for the defense. It is true that when it comes to professional services, one gets what one pays for. The generalization has been applied to socialized medicine in Great Britain, which is not to suggest that practitioners in the British Health Service are incompetent or that public hospitals or clinics dispense inadequate medical care. It indicates an awareness that in medicine, as in all things, that which is not poor may be graded as good, better, best. This is true whether it is the skills of the physician or surgeon, or the equipment, nursing care, diet, etc. of the hospital or clinic.

The same kinds of generalizations may be distilled from observations of legal services. Counsel need not be judged incompetent in the appellate courts to have provided less than quality legal service. As in many professional fields, the only thing that a lawyer has to sell are his skills and his time. If his goal is financial success, he sells them dearly. The typical criminal defendant cannot afford to retain counsel at all, let alone choose between better or best. Even with those highly competent professionals who give financial success a lower priority, there is always too much to be done. Large caseloads dictated by absence of fees are the enemy of quality service whether in the public health clinic or the public defender's office.

Equalilty before the law remains an ideal, probably unattainable, as long as: (1) the capabilities of individual lawyers vary; (2) the amounts of time that they have available for cases vary; and (3) as long as defendants are free to retain their own attorneys in accordance with their own private means. It is simply unrealistic to pretend to equality under the law when one defendant is represented by a nationally known, highly successful criminal trial advocate (or even a local luminary, for that matter) while another is represented by an overworked public defender who has only a fraction of his time, and few if any auxilliary services to bring to the case. Given a choice, you would probably not ponder for long a selection between these two alternatives.

Proposals for Additional Institutional Improvements   Inequalities in the defense of various individuals confronted by accusations of crimes do not appear to trouble us greatly. Beyond the provisions for some public defenders in response to slowly evolving rights to counsel, we have done little that is substantial to correct the situation and there have been few suggestions for additional improvement. Some have called for the development of preinsured legal services, in which the consumer reserves the right to retain his own attorney. To begin with, indigent defendants are too poor to pay insurance premiums. Furthermore, they would no doubt be classified as high-risk, high-premium clients. Since most criminal defendants have limited incomes, legal insurance offers little hope for solving the problem of unequal representation. More radical solutions such as socialized legal services seem to be highly unlikely. Even if such an approach could be made palatable to those who oppose it, the reservation of the right to pay for one's own privately retained attorney would undercut equality of representation. Those who could afford it would be eager to pay premium prices for the highly specialized services of the freelancer with the preferred track record.

Equality before the law is only an ideal to be striven for; it can never be an absolute reality. The justice system can hardly be more perfect than the society whose values it expresses or whose needs it serves. Consequently, cases are tried and punishment is meted out unequally. We cannot throw up our hands in despair over our defects and abandon the community to the crimes of the offender. Therefore, we must tolerate an imperfect system of justice in deference to the needs of society. But capital punishment is not so easily justified. Because it is irrevocable and so severe, it cannot be fairly compared with other penalties. The question is whether individuals should be expected to pay with their lives when they have been tried and sentenced by a defective, unjust system. A deep regard for human life should compel us to consider the death penalty with humility and great care. It is time to consider the issue directly.

Capital Punishment Cases and Discrimination in the 1970s

Furman v. *Georgia* was decided in 1972. The U.S. Supreme Court struck down the Georgia death penalty statute on constitutional grounds by a 5 to 4 vote of a deeply divided Court. The issue of capital punishment has divided the nation for decades and the Supreme Court mirrored that divisiveness in *Furman*. Each of the nine justices felt compelled to write a separate concurring or dissenting opinion.

Of the five justices who concurred in invalidating the Georgia statute, only two firmly agreed that the death penalty was itself cruel and unusual, and therefore always unconstitutional under the Eighth Amendment. Justice Marshall argued that capital punishment does not deter, is excessive, and repugnant to enlightened public opinion. (Marshall was unconvinced by the increasing favorable attitude toward capital punishment revealed in contemporary public opinion polls. He distinguished *enlightened* public opinion—based on a knowledge and understanding of the operations and social effects of capital punishment—from public opinion expressive of underlying vengeful motives.) Justice Brennan proposed four tests to gauge the cruelty and unusualness of punishment. To be considered constitutional a punishment: (1) cannot by its severity downgrade human dignity; (2) cannot be wholly arbitrary; (3) cannot be totally rejected by society; and (4) must not be patently unnecessary. In Justice Brennan's view, capital punishment fails on all four counts, and is unquestionably cruel and unusual. Justice Douglas was the only opinion writer who focused on discrimination as a central constitutional disability of the death penalty. For Douglas, the clear empirical fact of a discriminatory pattern in the application of the death penalty rendered it cruel and unusual and thus unconstitutional.

Justices White and Stewart had come to be identified as "swing men" on the Burger Court in criminal justice cases. They often cast critical votes, sometimes with the liberals, other times with the conservatives. Their votes to overturn the Georgia statute were essential in the *Furman* case. (Four years later in the *Gregg* case, Justice Potter Stewart would write the opinion of the Court sustaining a revised Georgia death penalty statute.) Justice White explicitly rejected the argument that the constitutionality of the death penalty itself was an issue before the court in *Furman*. Instead he focused on the infrequency of the application of the death penalty. Citing his own personal experience in the justice system, White could see no social ends that were being served by the death penalty's administration. Justice White's position implied that if the death penalty were more consistently applied, and proven to deter effectively, he might be able to sustain it. Justice Stewart found ample evidence that the death penalty was being arbitrarily administered, although he was not persuaded that there was evidence of discrimination as such.

Justice Douglas's opinion requires further comment. While Douglas asserted that the death penalty was cruel and unusual as it was presently being employed, he drew upon the empirical fact of past and existing patterns of racial discrimination. Several students of the *Furman* case have rightly judged that Justice Douglas's rationale is then not really an Eighth Amendment cruel and unusual argument. Instead, they insist that it is essentially a Fourteenth Amendment denial of due process and denial of equal protection of the laws argument. As shall later be elaborated, the position that the law is selective or discriminatory need not be restricted to its past or present administration. It is possible to extrapolate from past and present patterns of operation to predict future applications with a high degree of probability. Justice Douglas's opinion did not do so, however.

It is difficult to understand how almost all of the justices of the Supreme Court could reject or ignore the not inconsiderable evidence of discrimination. To begin with, there are the routine day-to-day operations of the criminal justice system itself. Given the deficiencies of the system as discussed, the data below is to be expected.

The Selectivity of the Death Penalty

The probability of being executed for murder is extremely low. It is estimated that about ten percent of the murders committed in this country qualify for the death penalty. At that rate, about 2,000 murders could have been tried as capital cases in 1982. Meanwhile, through 1983, the actual number of post-*Gregg* executions per year has been somewhat less than two, if 1977 is included. On that basis, the probability of being executed for capital murder is less than two in 2,000. If a realistic limit of 15 executions per year is projected, the chance of being executed for a capital murder would still only be 15 in 2,000 or approximately one in 137. These odds are disturbing for two reasons. First, because they strongly suggest that death is an unusual penalty for capital murder. The Supreme Court is unwilling to place any statistical connotation on the word *unusual*. It is difficult to discern what other criterion they might employ. Even if the word unusual is defined by reference to the synonym *odd,* there is a statistical or quantitative connotation. What is odd or *abnormal* is defined with reference to a *norm.*

Equally disturbing about the small number of executions is the process of selection. It really ought to trouble us greatly that so few of those sentenced to death out of a much larger number actually end up on the executioner's block. Why these and not others? Is it no more than happenstance? Or is it as Justice Stewart wrote, because of some kind of omniscience exercised by civilized juries in reserving the death penalty for only those most deserving cases? There may be some element of chance in the final selection. Limitation to so few may even reflect our ambivalence about the death penalty. Our reservation of the death penalty for so few is unlikely to be either wise or fair, as Justice Stewart implies in *Gregg.* It is far more likely that it is the result of discrimination. Consider the following data.

Discrimination Against Blacks

Some statisticians have reconstructed data on executions in the United States that predate national sources. The University of Alabama and the Interuniversity Consortium for Political and Social Research at the University of Michigan are presently engaged in a massive computerized aggregation of data on over 14,000 state ordered executions from colonial to present times. At present, however, completely reliable data are available only from 1930 onward. In that year, data on executions, death row populations, etc. began to appear in the National Prisoner Statistics. That compilation has since been published annually by various federal government bureaus. Between 1930 and the end of 1983, there were 3,870 officially recorded executions in the United States, including 11 in the post-moratorium period that began in 1977. Sixty percent of all executions have taken place in the South, with 9 percent in Georgia alone. Through 1967, 54 percent of all executions in the United States were of black persons, 1 percent of other minorities, and the remaining 45 percent of those executed were white.

The application of the death penalty in the crime of rape affords stark confirmation of discriminatory patterning. The U.S. Supreme Court excluded capital punishment for rape in *Coker v. Georgia* in 1977. The historical record prior to the moratorium in 1967 was appalling. While only 12 percent of all executions between 1930 and 1967 were for crimes of rape (most were for murder), 90 percent of all persons executed for rape were black. It should be emphasized that capital punishment for rape was largely employed in the southern or border states and that most blacks who were executed had been convicted of raping white women. The inference that racial discrimination was characteristic of executions for rape is consistent with the historical pattern of American race relations as well.

The modern record of Military Court Martials has been at least as bad as that of the criminal courts. Since 1952, 12 American military personnel have been executed. Anti-capital punishment groups have established that at least eight of these persons were black. While they admit that records are unclear in the other four cases, they insist that probably these individuals were black as well. The issue has been highlighted by the case of Wyatt L. Matthews, a 26-year-old black Army private sentenced to death for the rape-murder of an officer's wife in a base library in West Berlin in 1979. No one has been executed under the military's death penalty since 1962. Thus, the Matthew's case provided the first post-*Furman* test of the military's death penalty provisions. Incidentally, Matthew's IQ tested out at 64. Nevertheless, an Army psychiatrist testified that Matthews was only "mildly retarded" and could be held responsible for his crime. The normal range of intelligence is considered to be between 90 and 110. A quotient of 64 would appear to imply a level of function somewhat more than "mildly" impaired. In *U.S.* v. *Matthews,* decided in October 1983, the U.S. Court of Military Appeals ruled that sentencing provisions in the Uniform Code of Military Justice did not conform to guidelines enunciated by the Supreme Court in *Furman* and the 1976 landmark cases. In January 1984, new regulations to remedy the Code's defects were promulgated by Executive Order.

A number of researchers have sought to determine the significance of black/white execution ratios in more definite ways. They have carefully controlled variables that might alternatively explain the discrepancies on some basis other than race. The proportions of murders or rapes committed by blacks and whites, the presence of factors that aggravate or mitigate the degree of responsibility of the offender in the crime, etc. have been controlled. These more definite studies support the inference that racial discrimination has operated in the imposition of the death penalty.

The Wolfgang-Riedel Study

A particularly extensive study was conducted by criminologists Marvin Wolfgang and Marc Riedel of the Center for Studies in Criminology and Criminal Law at the University of Pennsylvania. In 1967, Wolfgang and Riedel studied the racial aspect of rape and the death penalty in 11 southern and border states. Such states had historically imposed the bulk of the death sentences for rape. Data was gathered on over 3,000 rapes in 230 counties which contained about 50 percent of the population in those 11 states. Subsequently, for the purpose of providing evidence for Legal Defense Fund attorneys in the capital punishment case of *Maxwell* v. *Bishop* in 1970, data on seven states were analyzed in detail. The findings summarized below were distilled from data on Alabama, Arkansas, Florida, Louisiana, Georgia, South Carolina, and Tennessee. The findings strongly supported the inference of racial discrimination in the imposition of capital punishment in rape cases: nearly seven times as many blacks received the death penalty for rape as did whites. The researchers note that on a chance basis alone, such a disparity could have resulted in only one of a thousand cases. This indicates that the disproportionate number of blacks executed for rape is due to some factor other than bad luck. Again, blacks who raped white victims were sentenced to death 18 times more often than offenders in rapes involving any other combination of offenders and victims. This, too, is a highly improbable outcome on chance alone. A number of other studies have reached similar conclusions.

Discrimination on the Basis of Victim's Race

Incidentally, the race of the *victim* as a selective factor in the imposition of the death penalty has never been directly considered by the U.S. Supreme Court, despite the existence of studies on the matter. However, in December 1983, the Court did order a stay in Georgia's execution of the death sentence of Alpha Otis Stephens. The stay was granted in order to allow the U.S. Court of Appeals for the 11th Circuit to hear arguments on the admissability of a study of sentencings in Georgia by David Baldus and his colleagues from the University of Iowa. The Court of Appeals is concerned only with the relevance of the data, since the Federal District Court in a different case is already considering the factual question of racial discrimination in the application of the Georgia death penalty statute.

In a *New York Times* News Service syndicated article (*Cincinnati Enquirer,* January 8, 1984), Fay S. Joyce discusses a recent eight-state study on death sentences and the race of the victim. Samuel Gross and Robert Mauro of Stanford University reviewed 17,000 homicides that resulted in 340 death sentences in seven southern and border states and in Illinois between 1976 and 1980. Joyce reports that while Gross and Mauro found that in each of the eight states the death penalty was more probable when the victim was white, and it was even more probable in Georgia and Florida. In Georgia, the death penalty was imposed in 6.7 percent of the slayings of whites, as opposed to only 0.9 percent of those cases in which the victim was black. In Florida, the percentages were 6.3 and 0.8 respectively. The University of Iowa and Stanford University studies only more fully and systematically document the conclusions of earlier, more restricted researches.

The Factor of Race, Post-Gregg

To return to the matter of discrimination in the race of the offender, rather than the victim; since the end of the moratorium, through June of 1984, a majority of the 20 persons who have been executed were white. In some cases, these white persons did not fight their execution to the bitter end. The post-*Gregg* experience with actual execution is virtually nonexistent. It is far too limited to permit generalization. However, data comparing pre- and post-*Gregg* death row populations permit some tentative inferences to be drawn in regard to more recent racial patterns.

In 1968, the year after the moratorium began, there were 520 inmates on death rows around the country. By 1973, a year after the *Furman* decision, that number declined to 130 as a result of that case. By 1975, a year prior to *Gregg,* the number had climbed to almost 500 again as commitments increased under newly revised statutes. Finally, a Legal Defense Fund study in April 1982 put the number of death row inmates at 1,005 in 33 of the 36 death penalty jurisdictions then existing. In January 1983, there were 1,137 inmates on death rows around the country and by the end of 1983, the death row population approximated 1,200. No doubt, the numbers will continue to rise, barring some radical increase in the rate of executions. The South continues to lead the nation in death row statistics. As late as 1980, seventy percent of those condemned to death were in Southern states. In January 1983, Florida, Texas, and Georgia combined had 460 inmates on death row. Only California, with 118 inmates on death row (and tied with Georgia for third place), approached these three Southern states.

Prior to the *Furman* decision, slightly over 50 percent of death row inmates were black. The 1982 Legal Defense Fund data indicated that blacks now composed only 40.6 percent of death row inmates. At first glance, it would appear that recent U.S. Supreme Court decisions limiting the discretion of juries in capital cases has impacted on arbitrariness and thus on racial discrimination. However, two considerations must be taken into account.

First, the 1982 data on death row proportions reflect some fallout from the 1977 *Coker* decision. The *Coker* decision no doubt had a very real impact on death row black/white ratios since a significant proportion of all executions were for rape and almost all of those executed for rape were black. From 1930 through 1967, 12 percent of all executions were for the crime of rape. Since 90 percent of those executed for rape were black, black persons executed for the crime of rape accounted for 10.8 percent of *all* persons executed over that thirty-year period. Meanwhile, a parallel set of data indicate that executions for rape account for just over 5 percent of all black executions (the remaining executions of blacks were for other offenses, primarily for murder). This 5 percent is roughly equivalent to one half of the total percentage decrease for blacks on death row prior to *Furman* in 1972 and 1982. Caution must be exercised in comparing these two sets of data because the time frames vary considerably. Still, the black/white proportion on death row has no doubt been affected in two ways by the *Coker* decision. First, commutations of the death sentences of blacks for rape would have decreased their numbers on death row. Second, the flow of blacks to death row would have been diminished somewhat in the five years after the *Coker* decision.

There is a second consideration that must enter into any evaluation of the impact of the *Gregg* decision on death row black/white proportions. It must also be borne in mind that data on executions are not exactly equal to death row figures. The death penalty has operated selectively at every stage in the criminal justice process from accusation through execution; not all of those condemned to death are ultimately executed. The percentage of all black executions is likely to be higher in the future than the percentage of all black inmates on death row. Several decades of post-*Gregg* experience will be required to fully assess the eventual impact of that decision on racial variations in the application of capital punishment.

Parallel Data: Local Studies

Nevertheless, there are other kinds of data that offer little basis for optimism. Recent studies in localized jurisdictions do not lead to the same tentative conclusions that might be drawn from small recent declines in the proportions of blacks on death rows. In Houston's Harris County, a recent study revealed that 65 percent of the cases in which blacks or Chicanos had murdered whites were tried as capital offenses. At the same time, only 25 percent of the cases where minority group persons were victimized by white offenders were tried as capital cases. A study of local jurisdictions in South Carolina yielded a similar pattern. Thirty-eight percent of the homicides in which offenders were black and victims white were tried as capital offenses. Only 13 percent of white killers were tried as capital offenders when the victims were black.

Such findings are consistent with those of a number of studies into race and capital punishment conducted prior to the Supreme Court's attempt to limit arbitrariness in the *Gregg* case. An extensive study of homicides in Philadelphia in 1970 is a notable example of pre-*Gregg* research into the racial factor. Again, black offenders were much more vulnerable to conviction for capital crimes than white offenders, particularly when their victims were white.

Such studies not only challenge the belief that the *Gregg* decision will appreciably reduce discrimination. They also indicate that racial discrimination will continue to play a role in the imposition as well as in the execution of the death penalty. Finally, the Houston and South Carolina studies, among others, point up the critical role of the prosecutor in the choice of capital punishment. In those jurisdictions prosecutors apparently chose to prosecute black offenders on capital charges much more frequently when victims were white. This inference is also consistent with those from earlier studies that emphasized the vulnerability of minority groups and other unpopular defendants to community pressures.

Summary: Race in the Historical Pattern of Executions

In general, the historical pattern is obvious. The black population, comprising 10 to 12 percent of the population over the time period covered, has suffered the death penalty more than half of the time that it has been inflicted. It may be argued by some that the result is consistent with the disproportionately higher homicide ratio for blacks in American society. The contention is without foundation. Careful studies indicate that even taking that factor into consideration, there remains ample evidence of discrimination. Moreover, the death penalty is supposed to be reserved for aggravated or first degree murders. It is not meant to punish random acts of violence even when they are homicides. It cannot be established that blacks have committed four to five times the number of aggravated murders in proportion to the general black population.

Homicide data are gathered without reference to the varying degrees of legal responsibility or severity of offenses. Even if such figures could be factored out to isolate first degree or aggravated murders, they would be of little value. They would still fail to account for the differences that affect sentences in the criminal justice process. As noted earlier, discretion exists at various critical points in the system. The discretion of prosecutors in charging, bargaining, and seeking alternative penalties is relatively unfettered. Even at the level of judge or jury, although the statutes now guide discretion in sentencing by specifying aggravating and mitigating circumstances, there is no control over biases in the guilt determination process itself. Moreover, the application of evidence to the criteria for aggravation also permits of bias as well.

There is another obstacle to establishing that blacks commit such a disporportionately high percentage of aggravated murders (as some infer from the very high percentage of blacks executed). Our general data do not permit very definitive identification of offender characteristics. The data that are available do not, however, bear out the common misconception that blacks dominate violent crime categories. The massive, federally-sponsored National Crime Survey asked victims to identify characteristics of those who had acted against them. As late as 1977, 70 percent of offenders in single offender violent crimes were identified as white, 25 percent as black, and 5 percent by other race. It is conceivable that racial prejudice could have had some influence on victim perceptions of offenders or on their reports to the survey, i.e., that victims overidentified blacks as offenders. Aside from that possibility, it is highly interesting to speculate on the racial selectivity of the criminal justice system.

Race and Poverty Linked as Factors

Aside from race, there is an additional factor not directly shown in NPS data. Case studies on death row inmates indicate that whatever their racial origins, the condemned are invariably society's losers. They are poorer, less educated, if not less intelligent, less employable, and frequently they manifest abnormal emotional characteristics and alcohol and other substance abuse patterns. In short, as a collection, they closely resemble their brethren in the general population of the penal institution.

The bulk of criminal justice system clients are poor and black who are disproportionately represented in the system. Death row inmates are among the poorest. Homicide is among the most universal of criminal acts. Felony murders, contract murders, murders by rejected lovers, betrayed or estranged spouses, murders by enraged neighbors, even murders of children by parents and vice versa indicate the range of homicide. The crime of homicide is not only bisexual, it is multi-classed as well. In the complexity of the capital trial, overshadowed by the awfulness of the death penalty, the highly-skilled, well-paid criminal trial advocate is in his element. Nowhere are his gifts of such immense importance as in pretrial maneuvering or in pleading in capital cases. Nowhere else are all of the subtle social attitudes that create sympathy for or antipathies to a defendant so significant.

Ambivalence to Death Penalty

Capital punishment brings together a number of critical factors that result in a process of social selection that is detrimental to black and poor people. To begin with, an ambivalence about capital punishment—a love-hate relationship to it—predisposes its limited use. On one side, capital punishment serves a variety of our needs: for revenge against the wrongdoer and for repression of those who defy authority. It quells our frustrations, engendered by the senselessness and wanton infliction of pain and suffering. It stifles the fear that arises as we go about uneasily in an unsafe society. Paradoxically, the death penalty may affirm our concerns about the value of human life.

On the other side, the death penalty is so terrible a punishment that we shrink from it; it repels civilized sentiments. Only the ghoul would wish for public execution today. As Justice Potter Stewart suggested, the infrequency of executions today may well reflect a growing sense of the severity of the death penalty and a civilized society's desire to restrict its use to only a few necessary cases.

What is particularly disquieting about such restrictions is that a disproportionately large number of such cases involve blacks and almost all of them involve the poor (or like the Rosenbergs, involve highly unpopular causes). Our squeamishness about the death penalty may well reflect our growing awareness of its awfulness. It may also reflect our unwillingness to apply it to those with whom it is easier for us to identify. Middle-class, white-collar offenders strike sympathetic chords in the breasts of middle-class judges and jurors. Respectability, common values, and common universes of discourse make it more difficult to perceive the offender as a criminal, and easier to define his misbehavior as an aberrant episode.

Our repugnance about capital punishment inclines us to resist applying it to those who elicit our sympathy. We are more detached about the application of the death penalty to those for whom we have little sympathy or feel outright antipathy. The far more extensive use of the death penalty in the South, with its almost exclusive imposition on blacks and poor whites, is consistent with the social attitudes that historically prevailed in that region. It is the few who have been required to bear the burden that is distasteful to us all.

Compounding Social Justice

The injustice in inflicting the death penalty almost exclusively on the poor and minority people is compounded by the reality that these are precisely the groups from whom we ought to expect the least. It is they who have received the least of our economy's bounty. They have suffered benign neglect if not outright deprivation of their material needs. It is these segments of society that have suffered most from social injustice. They have resided in squalid, rat-infested slums, surrounded by criminal influences. They have benefitted least from the civilizing environments many of us take for granted. The imposition of capital punishment on a disproportionate number of lower class people, particularly minorities, is a cruel irony indeed. Are we incapable of recognizing the perpetuation of injustice in that?

There is no excuse for inhuman behavior; society has no choice but to protect itself against the violent offender. There are, however, different ways to do it and varying degrees of responsibility. It is an inept society that has plenty, yet permits a significant segment of its people to live in relative economic and cultural deprivation. Uncivilized behaviors are consistent with uncivilized conditions of life. It is also a cynical, selfish society that then permits the death penalty to be largely reserved for those who have derived the least benefit from society.

These are moral realities. They cannot be simply dismissed as effusions of a bleeding heart. Capital punishment is unjust. It magnifies the social injustice that characterizes the way of life of the most materially blessed society in all history. It also magnifies the routine dificiencies of the "justice" system. Poor people, many of whom bear the additional burden of minority identification, are less likely to elicit sympathy from officials in the justice system, jurors, or the community. (It is interestng to conjecture how long the death penalty would have lasted in America if the overwhelming percentage of the executed had been typically middle-class. Witness, e.g., our growing social and legal tolerance of marijuana possession and use as they spread into the middle classes.) Supreme Court decisions have sought to control arbitrariness by limiting discretion in the sentencing process. There is, however, little control over guilt determination processes or over the options of prosecutors in charging or plea bargaining.

Inevitability of Inequalities

It is a social and political reality that these deficiencies are not likely to disappear. Social "progress" is only a theory; it is not an accomplished fact. This side of the millenium, social class divisions will always persist. Differences in power will always exist. Inequalities before the law will always exist. They are predicated on our belief in the necessity and rightness of class divisions and on the self-interest which such divisions engender. Perfect justice is an ideal to be striven for. It is the most fundamental of all social values and virtues. It is worth all of the effort expended in its behalf. We cannot anticipate a perfectly just society, but can continue to make an effort. The abolition of capital punishment is a realistic, attainable milestone along the pathway to a just society.

QUESTIONS FOR REFLECTION AND DISCUSSION

1. Discuss various evidences of continuing tensions between lower class, minority people and community agencies, particularly the police.

2. How do our perceptions of crime affect public opinion, and the way in which the law is enacted, enforced, adjudicated, and satisfied through punishment?

3. Consider the alleged discrimination against blacks in the imposition and execution of the death penalty in the general context of the history of race relations in the U.S.

4. How might the exercise of discretion discussed in earlier chapters link up with the factors of racial selection discussed in this chapter?

5. If the thesis of this chapter is rejected consider alternative explanations for the facts given.

6. Consider the factors usually employed to define aggravated or first degree murder (e.g., murder of a police officer, in the commission of a felony, the heinous nature of the crime, etc.). Do you agree or disagree with the parity assigned among such factors?

CHAPTER FIVE

THE DETERRENCE QUESTION BEFORE 1975

On January 23, 1984, National Public Radio's "All Things Considered" newscast carried a report on the current state of capital punishment in the Chinese People's Republic. A reporter in residence spoke of an outbreak of executions of young people for such civil crimes as murder, rape, and burglary during the preceding six months. NPR reported varying estimates that somewhere between five and twenty thousand persons had been shot during that period. Apparently, Chinese authorities have been concerned about Westernization and rapidly escalating crime rates among the young, which they attribute to it. (In a 1977 article in the *Journal of Criminal Law and Criminology,* Hungdah Chiu reported that Chinese law inclined to extensive use of the death penalty. He was particularly alerted by the vagueness of the statutes that permitted broad discretion to bureaucratic officials.)

The frequent public use of capital punishment is intended to deter young people from engaging in criminal behavior. School children are assembled and required to witness executions that are multiple and summary in nature. A bizarre deterrent twist is imparted to the grisly proceedings by billing the parents of offenders for the cost of the bullet used to dispatch their offspring.

Certainly, all the elements of deterrence considered so essential by its proponents are present in the Chinese experience. Executions are frequent, swift, public, and apparently certain. Still, despite official reports of deterrent consequences, crime rates remain at high levels. The long-range impact on the crime rate cannot be determined. In any event, American public opinion would be unlikely to countenance such a barbaric application of the death penalty even in the name of deterrence, and even with its pro-capital punishment bias.

To refocus on the United States, what is so tragic about the injustices of capital punishment is that they are done as in China in the name of community protection. Some who might have reservations about capital punishment would nevertheless tolerate miscarriage of justice, discriminatory applications of the law, etc. on the grounds that the death penalty might deter offenders from wreaking havoc on innocent persons. There are at least two responses to that contention. First, as Hugo Bedau once asked, how many rights can the community require the individual person to sacrifice in its own interest? Second, there is no real evidence that capital punishment does deter. This second consideration occupies the bulk of the present chapter; the first may be dispensed with briefly.

Community Protection and Individual Rights

The relative priorities of the common good and the rights of the individual present a classic problem in social philosophy and public policy. A tradition as old as Aristotle defines the common good to be the sum total of those conditions that would permit the individual to realize his or her potential as a human person. Aristotle saw no real conflict between the individual and the commonwealth; he saw the two as indivisible and interdependent. The community existed for the individual, not for itself. In his own interest as well as in the interests of others, the individual therefore had obligations to promote the common good. Aristotle defined the purpose of the state to be promotion of this good life.

Social philosophers and jurists have distinguished priorities or orders of rights. Thus, the right to life or the right to liberty are considered more important then the right to own or use private property. The hue and cry in response to Mayor Daley's policy pronouncements in the midst of the tumult in Chicago in 1968 offers a case in point. His orders to shoot and kill looters sparked indignation across the land, indicative of the degree to which our society favors life over property. Paradoxically, some complain bitterly of governmental limits on private enterprise and call loudly for economic freedom from government intervention at the same time they complain of constitutional limits on governmental power over those caught up in the criminal justice system. They resent government scrutiny of and restrictions on the activities of powerful economic corporations, yet see no tyranny in denying protection to individuals accused, tried, convicted, and punished by government.

For all of the difficulties that these extensions of constitutional guarantees present to criminal justice functionaries, we have seen what happens in their absence. The storm trooper-like tactics of federal narcotics agents with their night-time raids on private residences (sometimes at the wrong addresses) led to the eventual repeal of the "no knock" provisions of the narcotic control laws. They also highlight the dangers to privacy and the intimidation factor which Fourth Amendment limitations on search and seizure seek to prevent. Flagrant denials of privacy rights such as extorted or tricked confessions, violations of fair trial procedures, etc. not only undermine the fundamental burden on the state to establish the guilt of the accused beyond a reasonable doubt, but they seriously incommode and sometimes jeopardize the innocent.

Some critics chafe under what they deem to be an excess of constitutional nicety on the part of Supreme Court civil libertarians. They not only prejudge the accused as guilty, they would have us sacrifice those rights of individuals to protect the community. In the same way, some would argue that in the interest of deterrence, we must execute more frequently and more swiftly than we do at present. This, in accord with the classic theory of criminal deterrence developed by Bentham, Beccaria, and other utilitarian reformers who hold that the deterrent value of a punishment is relative to its severity, celerity, and certainty.

Capital Punishment and Deterrence

Before examining those conditions of effective deterrence more close-ly, the distinction between deterrence and other means of crime prevention should be made. Deterrence is only one way to prevent criminal behavior. The imprisonment and the rehabilitation of the offender are other means of crime prevention. Crime may be cur-tailed through preventive means such as drying up the illegal drug market, or affixing permanent identification to property items. Crime may also be prevented by reducing crime-producing conditions, by reducing unemployment in the community.

The preventive force of deterrence is found in the threat of punishment. It is predicated on the utilitarian principle that human behavior is oriented to maximizing pleasure and avoiding pain. Pro-ponents of capital punishment will argue that the swift administra-tion of the death penalty as well as its certainty are essential if the death penalty is going to be an effective deterrent. The early utilitarians did not lay as much emphasis on the severity of punish-ment as do comtemporary advocates of capital punishment. Indeed, the nineteenth-century reformers generally opposed capital punish-ment, instead emphasizing the necessity for punishment to be swift and certain rather than predominantly severe.

The Argument for Deterrence: Swiftness and Certainty   While proponents of capital punishment generally insist that capital punish-ment *does* deter, they nonetheless hedge their bets on the matter. First, like the scholar Ernest van den Haag, some will argue that the absence of evidence that capital punishment deters does not prove that it *doesn't* deter. In that case, neither does the absence of such evidence prove that it *does* deter. Second, proponents of capital punishment will argue that capital punishment could be an effective deterrent only if it were more certainly and more swiftly ad-ministered. In other words, even capital punishment advocates are willing to admit in a lefthanded way that the penalty is an unusual one. They do not, however, identify the source of infrequent use to be our own ambivalence and misgivings about the death penalty. Rather they place the blame for both delay and uncertainty on the judicial process. The villains in the piece are those appellate court judges, particularly in the federal system, who entertain numerous appeals and overturn convictions and sentences on legal technicalities.

If only the federal courts would cease their intrusions into state criminal justice proceedings, more people could be executed with greater dispatch making the death penalty more effective.

The contention is an assertion, or at best, a hypothesis. It is, of course, virtually uncontestable under current operational conditions. Swiftness as a variable in the deterrent effectiveness of capital punishment has never been studied. Little support for the hypothesis that capital punishment would exhibit deterrence if it were more certain has been provided by research. William Bailey's 1974 study of rape and the death penalty was exceptional in that it sought to assess the deterrent effect of the certainty factor in executions. Comparing retentionist and abolitionist states from 1944 to 1967, Bailey sought, among other things, to determine whether rape rates were lower in retentionist states with higher execution rates for rape. Bailey found that differences in rape rates among the retentionist states were insignificant; the hypothesis that certainty of execution increases deterrence was not confirmed by his data.

Publicity and Deterrence   While it is virtually impossible to determine conclusively whether swiftness and certainty enhance deterrence, the historical record offers little support for the hypothesis. Public administration of punishment did not help either. (Stories of pickpockets working among crowds of revelers at public executions are well known.) The maintenance of a "rogue's gallery" or dishonor roll of executees in the Ohio death house is anachronistic. It is a bit too macabre for modern sensibilities. Lew Moores (*Cincinnati Post,* Feb. 23, 1982) writes that a member of the Georgia legislature recently proposed that his state employ a mobile death house. It was his idea that a prominently identified van should move about the state executing felons in the locales of their offense and conviction. He reasoned that the grim presence of such a death vehicle would strike terror in the hearts of other potential capital offenders and thus deter them from the commission of such crimes. Apparently his brainchild was a bit much even for a state that has the dubious distinction of leading the nation in the use of capital punishment. It has yet to be implemented.

Nonutilitarian Considerations of Deterrence

In all of this discussion about deterrence, utility and speed, certainty and publicity, it is easy to forget that we are not discussing the cost-effective operation of a slaughterhouse. We are dealing with considerations of human life. No matter what an individual is alleged to have done, is convicted of doing, or for that matter is guilty of doing, the person remains a human being. Humanity is not negated by behavior. We do not go about assigning degrees of humanness to one another. In affirming the humanness of others, we affirm our own. Communal fears and the drive to protect ourselves, no matter how legitimate, should not incline us to deny the rights of others. It is all too simple and alluring to ensure our own security at the expense of others. We must bear in mind, however, that if rights can be denied to any one of us, no matter how guilty, they may also be denied to any of us, no matter how innocent.

Accelerate executions and make them more certain. Short-circuit the appeals process, foreclose access to the federal courts and close legal loopholes that result in overturned convictions and sentences, new trials, etc. Let stand convictions and death sentences arrived at in violation of due process or equal protection under the laws. How many rights must the individual sacrifice in order to guarantee the deterrent efficacy of capital punishment? At what point is society safe enough to permit halting this recommended erosion of constitutional safeguards? On the other hand, the true test of our pretensions to a just and humane way of life is to continue to ensure that individual rights are not forfeited to the insecurities and panic responses of the moment. Should the reader be tempted to dismiss the foregoing as platitudinous, he or she need only to remember, the excesses of the McCarthy era, the over-reaction to dissent in the 1960s and 70s, and the criminal actions in the Watergate affair by the guardians of law and order. These events did not really make us any more secure either.

The deterrent value of capital punishment is suspect, although its advocates appear to presume that the death penalty deters. They blame the lack of deterrence on the system's lack of speed and certainty in carrying out death sentences. It is time now to turn to the larger question: has the death penalty really served as the effective deterrent that its advocates have purported it to be?

Role of Deterrence in Social Control

At first glance, the concept of deterrence appears to be simple enough. Deterrence is one form of crime prevention that functions through the threat of punishment. It presumes that human behavior is rational and that people assess the pros and cons of their acts beforehand. If the individual is otherwise prone to offend and if the punishment threatened is in excess of the value to be gained, he will be inclined to restrain himself, assuming that his assessment is a reasonable one. Without this assumption, the whole fabric of threat and self-restraint falls apart. For the purposes of analysis, the foregoing description may have idealized or overstated the rational element inherent in the utilitarian theory. Human behavior is complex and its conditioning is not simple.

Although the deterrence theory appears simple on the surface, there are several assumptions and implications in it that complicate it. To begin with, it should be recognized that most people conform to the law independent of any deterrent threat. They conform to laws as they conform to other kinds of social norms, to tradition, customs, and moral standards. They conform because they have been socialized in the community and are expected to conform; they have internalized the rules in question, and they believe in the *rightness* of them and the moral authority of the community to command. Moreover, most people are "normal," well-adjusted individuals, free of personality impairments which may play a role in deviant behavior for others. Indeed, a society could not exist at all if most of its members did not have an abiding allegiance to it. Punishment is intended in part, therefore, to deter those relatively few "unsocialized" individuals who might deviate from the law. Social solidarity and respect for the law and authority guarantee conformity. Coercion and repression are necessary only when the law lacks meaning and has only tenuous control over the behavior of individuals. In the latter case, where the state controls only through overt force or the veiled threat, there is a constant state of tension between it and its citizenry. The legitimacy of the law is repudiated by covert resistance or even sporadic outbursts of rebellion.

A second complication in the deterrence notion is that it is predicated on rational decision making on the part of the criminal. This principle presents at least two problems. First, observation of our own behavior and the behavior of others indicates that much of human action is not very rational. It is generally conceded that economic activity is the most rational sector of man's everyday behavior. Yet even here we find that man acts by habit or on impulse, emotion, hunches. Allowing sacred cows or monkeys to plunder the crops in a marginally subsistent economy is hardly rational. Even the meteoric rises and plummeting declines in the stock market are often in response to extraneous, ephemeral events.

People fall far short in reaching the utilitarian ideal of the "economic person." In terms of criminal deterrence, murder, assault, burglary, indecent exposure, nonprofit-oriented arson, vandalism, etc. are hardly rational.

The other problem with the notion of a person rationally considering a criminal act is, as Jack Gibbs and others have pointed out, that such an assessment actually involves the *perception* of the person, and not some set of objective facts. Perceptions may or may not correspond to facts, but they are generally more controlling. Thus, even if an individual were to assess the pros and cons prior to committing a crime, we must still wonder: what does he perceive to be the probability that he will be caught, and if caught, prosecuted and convicted, and if convicted, punished. (Incidentally, the reality of decreasing probabilities of arrest, prosecution, conviction, and punishment for crime is well borne out by official data at both the national and local levels.) In addition, what is his perception of the severity of the alternative punishment provided by law? In other words, deterrence is an objective intention implemented by a society in an effort to control crime, but it operates as a subjective state in the mind of the individual.

The Impact of Deterrence on Capital Crime

It is this fact that so frustrates our attempts to measure the deterrent values of punishment. We can only infer deterrence; we cannot measure it in any direct way. Consequently, when Mr. Justice Stewart implies in *Gregg* v. *Georgia* that capital punishment must have deterred someone, somewhere from committing capital crime, he is asserting an article of faith, not a proven fact. It is obvious that capital punishment did not deter the overwhelming numbers among the condemned who actually committed crimes. The death rows of the nation are beginning to overflow with the failures of the deterrent approach to capital crimes, just as our courts and correctional institutions are glutted with those who were not deterred from the commission of other kinds of crime. In every case where capital punishment has apparently failed to deter, the possibility exists that some unknown who has not murdered *was* deterred.

The only way in which deterrence can be satisfactorily measured and evaluated is statistically, i.e., in terms of group probabilities. If one jurisdiction has retained the death penalty and another has abandoned it, and if the jurisdictions are similar in major respects, then a statistical comparison is possible. If there are significantly fewer capital crimes in retentionist than in abolitionist jurisdictions, there is evidence of a marginally deterrent effect of capital punishment. Conversely, if retentionist jurisdictions do not have significantly fewer eligible offenses, there is no support for the hypothesis that the death penalty is a superior deterrent. An alternative strategy may be to compare similar before-and-after periods in states that have abolished or restored the death penalty. If homicide rates increase after abolition or decrease after initiation of the death penalty, it may be inferred that it is marginally deterrent. If homicide rates remain essentially unchanged, there is no evidence of marginal deterrence. Capital punishment studies have employed these basic approaches no matter how crude or sophisticated the methods and techniques applied. To date, no one has invented a more acceptable research strategy.

It was noted earlier that some proponents of capital punishment would still argue that the absence of evidence of deterrence does not mean that the death penalty does not deter. Certainly not, but there is no way to prove that something does not exist. Logically, all one can do is infer from the absence of evidence to the contrary that it does not exist. The burden of proof would nonetheless appear to rest on those who argue in support of existence. Reasonable people feel no compulsion to provide an absolute refutation of the existence of a possibility. They are content with the assumption that while something is always possible, it is improbable in the absence of supporting evidence. The nitty-gritty of the deterrence question is precisely that: does the weight of the evidence establish the probability that the death penalty is a better deterrent of capital crime than alternative punishment? It is enough to determine that. It is time to examine the evidence itself.

Deterrence Studies: Pre-1975

Deterrence research may be roughly divided into two periods, pre- and post-1975. The dividing line is by no means absolute. For example, a number of studies completed shortly before that date will be considered along with post-1975 research. The 1975 dividing line is not entirely temporal. It relates to differences in the approach and techniques used by the researcher. Research produced in the period before 1975, like that conducted by Edwin Sutherland, utilized a cross-sectional method. Retentionist and abolitionist states were compared on general homicide rates.

Logic of Research and Earlier Deterrence Studies   These earlier studies generally suffer from the simplicity of their methods. The experimental methods of the natural sciences can be only approximated in the social sciences. Social researchers are not in a position to exert absolute controls over their research subjects. While the techniques employed by researchers may be complicated, the logic of experimentation is fundamentally simple. Cancer researchers have studied the relationship between tobacco smoking and cancer in laboratory animals under carefully controlled conditions. They can carefully match *experimental* animals (those treated with tobacco) and *control* or untreated animals on biological traits (age, sex, size, maturation, inherited tendencies), and control the environments (diet, water, air) of both groups of animals to ensure that they are equivalent.

If the two groups of animals develop a similar number of cancers over time, the researchers may conclude that there is no evidence that tobacco administered under the conditions imposed by their experiment produces cancer in this particular species of animals. However, if the treated animals develop a significant number of cancers and the untreated develop none or very few, the researcher may infer the opposite. Since the biological and environmental conditions were controlled, they may be ruled out as alternative sources of cancer.

Even the laboratory methods of the natural sciences have their limits. For example, the transfer of data and conclusions on laboratory animals to human subjects is always questionable. Application of data on the effects of tobacco on test animals to humans stimulates debate about issues such as dosages relative to the size of the test animals, and tissue differences. Obviously, research in the social sciences is even more problematic since the researcher cannot manipulate variables in advance. More often than not, he is required to reverse the research process and proceed from effect (e.g., the homicide rate) to the cause (e.g., capital punishment or its absence). Thus, he must use the homicide rate as a control, *after the fact* of its occurrence.

Limitations of Early Studies   While there are reasonably effective techniques that permit such controls, they were not very well developed when the earliest capital punishment studies were done. The major deficiency of these earlier studies was that they made little attempt to consider demographic, social, and economic factors that could have affected homicide rates independently of the presence or absence of the death penalty. Consequently, differences between retentionist and abolitionist states on such characteristics as racial composition, rural and urban population, and income and employment levels, could very well have affected homicide rates and masked any real deterrent effects of the death penalty. These earlier attempts to assess the deterrent superiority of capital punishment invariably found just the opposite of predicted results. Homicide rates were *not lower* in retentionist states, but were consistently higher!

Later Improvements in Cross-Sectional Techniques   Later a number of researchers repeated such cross-sectional studies, imparting a slightly new twist in the methods employed. Thorstein Sellin was among the first to attempt to exert control over demographic, social, and economic variables. Sellin selected for comparison contiguous retentionist and abolitionist states (e.g., Ohio, Indiana, and Michigan) since such states would be similar in such factors as race, percentage of urban population, per capita income, and unemployment levels. The studies of Sellin and others who utilized this method again invariably found homicide rates to be higher in retentionist as opposed to abolitionist states.

Other Later Approaches   In 1952, Karl Schuessler reported on the result of his longitudinal study for 11 states between 1930 and 1949. He sought to test the "certainty" factor in deterrence by calculating the "risk" of executions (i.e., the number of executions per 1,000 homicides annually). He concluded that homicides and executions varied independently of one another. There was no evidence of deterrence, or that the risk of execution had any effect on the homicide rate. Nor could Schuessler find any evidence of increased homicide in several European countries after the abolition of capital punishment.

Thorstein Sellin was a pioneer in the development of cross-sectional deterrence studies. He also studied the death penalty's impact on general homicide rates with a longitudinal method. He compared general homicide rates in the same jurisdictions for similar periods before and after abolition or restoration of the death penalty. This longitudinal method would appear to be superior to the cross-sectional approach in at least one major respect: any jurisdiction could serve as its own control. Even this method could not entirely ensure that extraneous effects were not operating. The probability that demographic, social, and economic conditions were highly variable would be minimized over the short range by restricting the before-and-after time periods in the same state. Once again, Sellin could find no evidence that general homicide rates were reduced by the death penalty or were higher in its absence.

Summary of Findings

These findings were then perfectly consistent with those of other capital punishment deterrence studies conducted prior to 1975. Hugo Bedau, who has dedicated much of his academic career to the study of capital punishment, was prompted to observe in the early 1970s that despite constant attempts to justify the death penalty on deterrence grounds, there was not a shred of evidence that it did in fact deter.

Limitations of Findings

It should be emphasized at this juncture that research into the deterrent effects of capital punishment has hardly implemented rigid experimental designs. By necessity, deterrence research is macrosocial research which attempts to discern existing patterns in jurisdictions which can be only approximated to one another. Another technical problem with almost all deterrence studies is that they used general homicide rates as outcome measures. Capital punishment is not, however, directed to the deterrence of all homicides, but only that limited class of homicides that are often referred to today as aggravated and used to be called first degree homicides. In other words, capital punishment is intended to deter only those capital murders which are defined by law as most grave. It has been difficult to factor out such murders from general homicide data, which aggregate all homicides regardless of the degree of culpability within a given jurisdiction. Only one major study by William Bailey of the deterrent effect of the death penalty has attempted to limit its relationship directly to eligible homicides.

For these reasons, researchers are cautious about interpreting their results. Deterrence research has not yet passed beyond the pre-experimental or exploratory phase. That remains the case despite more careful and more methodologically sophisticated studies done by researchers like William Bailey in the period around 1975. Such necessary qualifications are not intended to impugn the veracity of earlier studies, or diminish the significance of their findings. Research prior to 1975 consistently failed to confirm the assumption and assertion that capital punishment deterred eligible crimes.

QUESTIONS FOR REFLECTION AND DISCUSSION

1.   Consider hypothetically how swift and certain the death penalty would have to be to produce an acceptable level of marginal deterrence.

2.   Discuss the relationship between moral development and conformity to law. How does this approach reflect on the rationalistic interpretation of human behavior?

3.   Can the possibility of a given penalty's deterrent effect on the individual be reconciled with an apparent lack of deterrence for the group?

4.   Can the argument that someone, somewhere, has been deterred from capital crime by the death penalty also be applied to alternative punishments like life imprisonment?

5.   Discuss the role of punishment as an affirmation of the rightness or goodness of moral or legal norms as opposed to direct deterrence or deviation from those norms.

6.   Discuss the differences between the research approaches of the natural and social sciences. What implications do these differences have for the standard of proof required on the capital punishment issue?

CHAPTER SIX

THE DETERRENCE QUESTION AFTER 1975

The preceding chapter outlined the findings of researchers working prior to 1975, which consistently failed to yield evidence of a marginally deterrent effect of capital punishment. That neat order was abruptly disturbed by the publication by an American economist of an article entitled, "The Deterrent Effect of Capital Punishment: A Question of Life or Death" in the June 1975 issue of the *American Economic Review*. Isaac Ehrlich's article broke new ground on at least two fronts. First, it challenged the general conclusions drawn from previous deterrence research by providing evidence of marginal deterrence by the death penalty. It also applied, for the first time in deterrence research, methods developed in modes of economic analysis. Moreover, it catalyzed reexamination of the issue from a number of vantage points.

Essentials of Ehrlich's Study

The mathematics of Ehrlich's econometric model are somewhat complex, but a basic understanding of his approach may be conveyed without destroying its integrity. Ehrlich proceeds from the utilitarian theory of punishment; he assumes that there are rational murderers who consider in advance the risks related to their behavior. Therefore, he hypothesized that the "elasticities" of the murder rate with three punishment variables (severity, certainty and swiftness) should all be negative and in order of decreasing magnitude.

Utilizing data for the entire United States between 1930 and 1967, Ehrlich attempted to take into account the probability of arrest for murder, the probability of conviction upon arrest, and the probability of execution upon conviction. He also attempted to control for various demographic and socio-economic variables such as the age distribution of the population, percentage of the nonwhite population, and unemployment rates. Ehrlich concluded that his data did confirm the hypothesis that the murder rate did vary inversely with the punishment variables over the time period studied. He also claimed that his data permitted the further extrapolation that every execution prevented 8 additional murders.

While this interpretation is considerably oversimplified, it preserves the essential integrity of Ehrlich's approach. In any event, the publication of Ehrlich's findings rekindled the debate between pro and anti-capital punishment forces. It also stimulated fresh research on deterrence, employing more careful methods. Ehrlich's research was carefully scrutinized and carefully repeated.

Reaction to Ehrlich's Work

A complete catalogue of the replications of Ehrlich's study and of the specific deficiencies of his research as alleged by his critics is beyond the scope and purpose of this writing. Suffice it to say, Ehrlich was widely criticized on the grounds of his assumptions about human behavior and the constancy of socioeconomic variables, deficiencies in his data base, and other aspects of his method. When his work was repeated by economists and other researchers who utilized his techniques or modifications of them, it failed. In 1978, the National Academy of Sciences negatively reviewed his research.

The work of Robert Hahn also has particular significance in the assessment of Ehrlich's findings. Hahn was commissioned by the office of the Canadian Solicitor General to evaluate Ehrlich's work in connection with the debates about capital punishment then underway in the Canadian Parliament. Hahn appraised Ehrlich's work in conjunction with the studies of a number of others who had employed econometric methods. His survey of the literature was quite thorough, even including a number of manuscripts unpublished up to that time. Hahn arrived at the same conclusions that a number of others had reached using methods similar to Ehrlich's: one could, using Ehrlich's techniques with different assumptions, data bases, etc. easily arrive at conclusions different, and even contradictory, to Ehrlich's.

A rare study might appear in the literature that offered some semblance of support for Ehrlich's observations. Nevertheless, the consensus that emerged out of repetitions of Ehrlich's study was that his findings were flawed. The purported deterrent effects of capital punishment remained unproven in the minds of most students of the problem. Other than Ehrlich's own subsequent work, only one published study offers some tentative support for part of Ehrlich's findings. Kenneth Wolpin analyzed data from England over the years 1929 to 1968. He related the crime control variables of clearance by arrest, conviction, and alternative punishments to homicide rates. He concluded that increasing the proportion of homicides cleared as murders, i.e., reducing the proportion cleared as manslaughters, decreased homicides. At the same time, he noted that *executions* of convicted murderers reduced homicides by only a small percentage. In short, deterrence is considerably increased by certainty of punishment; executions as such had little apparent effect. The Ehrlich study's value lay in the fact that it sparked an interest in deterrence research and stimulated improvements in the methods of conducting it. All the same, by the mid-1970s, when Ehrlich's capital punishment study appeared, other researchers were also looking at the issue in more sophisticated ways. A number were conducted with more developed and more careful techniques than those employed in earlier research.

Other Important Studies

Three studies that are particularly worthy of consideration are Zeisel's 1976 approximation of a natural experiment and Bailey's two studies of capital punishment as it relates to murder and rape. **Zeisel's Research**   The Zeisel study covered most of the moratorium period, utilizing data from the years 1967 to 1975. Zeisel took advantage of the moratorium on capital punishment to study the impact on homicide rates of the total absence of executions for a prolonged period. He reasoned that if homicide rates were to rise much more rapidly in retentionist than in abolitionist states in the absence of executions, the deterrent effect of the death penalty would be indicated. Zeisel found that homicide rates increased less in capital punishment states than in abolitionist states during the moratorium years studied. Therefore, there was no increase in capital offenses that could be related to the absence of executions in capital punishment states.

Reflecting on his own findings in relationship to those of other researchers, Zeisel couched his general conclusion in unusually strong language. He argued that the statistical evidence regarding deterrence was far from inconclusive. On the contrary, he asserted, the evidence overwhelmingly opposes the view that capital punishment deters.

Bailey's Study of Homicide and Capital Punishment   In the mid-1970s two unusually thorough and methodologically developed studies by William Bailey also addressed the deterrence issue. Bailey studied the purported deterrent effects of the death penalty on both murder and rape.

Capital punishment deterrence studies have been vulnerable to criticism in that they employ general homicide rates rather than restricting homicide to those eligible for the death penalty. In his homicide study, Bailey did not use these general rates. He went to unusual lengths to separate homicides into: (1) first degree murders; (2) second degree murders; (3) total murders; and (4) homicides. He compared capital punishment and abolitionist states on all four categories for 1967 and 1968. Bailey then conducted a number of stage by stage comparisons. His data indicated that for both years, rates in all four categories were subtantially higher for the capital punishment states taken as a whole than for the aggregate abolitionist states. When contiguous capital punishment and abolitionist states were compared, the same results were obtained in all four categories. Bailey then directly controlled his comparison of capital punishment and abolitionist states on two economic and five demograpic variables. The two economic factors were median family income and median education level. The five demographic factors were percentage nonwhite, percentage 18 to 24 years old, population size, population density, and percentage metropolitan. The results remained consistent. Capital punishment states still had higher first degree murder rates, second degree murder rates, total murder rates, and homicide rates.

Bailey's Study of Rape and Capital Punishment   Though not as thorough or developed as his study of homicide, Bailey's study of capital punishment and rape also affords some interesting and relevant findings. Bailey compared rape rates in capital punishment and abolitionist states for the period 1944 to 1967. In order to determine whether or not certainty of execution increased deterrent effects, he also compared rape rates to execution rates within capital punishment states. Bailey found that rape rates were considerably higher in retentionist states than in the abolitionist states. On the other hand, he did find that within retentionist states higher execution rates were correlated with lower rape rates for almost all of the years between 1944 and 1967. Nevertheless, almost all of the relationships were low negative and proved to be statistically insignificant. Bailey concluded that his findings on the deterrent effects of capital punishment on rape almost directly paralleled findings on homicide.

Lack of Evidence of Marginal Deterrence

It has been constantly reported here that the rates of eligible crimes are *not lower* but *higher* in capital punishment states. The facts clearly contradict the deterrence theory's prediction. It was also noted in passing that two quite different interpretations have been assigned to those facts. One school of thought asserts that capital punishment is a counter-deterrent rather than a deterrent—the death penalty *causes* capital crime. The other explanation posits a third factor: a lesser respect for life that is responsible for both higher homicide rates and capital punishment. No summary of the deterrent effects of the death penalty would be adequate without a review of these positions.

The Counter-Deterrence Theory   The case for the alleged counter-deterrent effects of capital punishment derives from clinical observations and a small number of quantitative studies. Some psychiatrists, relying on case histories like that of Gary Gilmore, have interpreted some murders as "suicides." When they are committed in capital punishment states, such murders are seen as consequences of pathological guilt and ultimate punishment seeking. Or they are seen as attempts to utilize the state as an instrument of suicide by persons who desire to die, but cannot inflict death upon themselves.

The basic problem with the clinical approach to counter-deterrence is that it is such a highly individualized approach. It suffers from the same limitation inherent in the subjective approach to deterrence. We can never be very certain about whether or not a given individual was deterred from the commission of a particular murder (or to put the matter into Mr. Justice Stewart's broader context, we can never be sure that someone somewhere may have been deterred.) Another difficulty with the counter-deterrence argument is that it may very well confuse a subcultural preoccupation with fate, characteristic of lower socioeconomic class offenders, with a preexisting death wish. It is interesting if not ironic to note, for example, that while Charlie Brooks, Jr.'s arm bore the tattooed legend, "Born to Die," he tenaciously resisted the state of Texas's efforts to take his life.

For such reasons, when we seek to determine the deterrent effects of capital punishment, we must go beyond individual factors and attempt to do so on a statistical basis. In the same way, quantitative studies have attempted to determine whether or not the death penalty has counter-deterrent effects. A number of researchers have compared homicide rates in periods just before and just after well-publicized executions or sentences of death. Only one supports the counter-deterrent theory to any extent. William Graves studied California executions in the period 1946 to 1948 when they were always carried out on Friday mornings. Graves found more homicides committed on those weekends when executions were held than on other weekends. Although the subject has not been researched exhaustively, most students of capital punishment either reject the counter-deterrence theory or suggest the need for additional careful research.

Capital Punishment, Higher Homicide Rates, and Devaluation of Life   In 1974, Daniel Glaser and Max Ziegler presented a novel alternative to the counter-deterrence theory. They sought to test it against their own hypothesis that frequent use of capital punishment and high homicide rates are *both* the result of devaluation of human life. They tested their theory by comparing the length of confinement for homicide in capital punishment and abolitionist states. Paradoxically, they found that the length of confinement for homicide was considerably less in retentionist states than in states that had abolished the death penalty. Moreover, the more executions conducted by a state, the shorter the period of imprisonment before parole for those not executed for homicide. These data led Glaser and Ziegler to conclude that: (1) the state's willingness to forgive killers, (2) capital punishment, and (3) the murder rate, all derive from a common cause—the devaluation of human life.

Glaser and Ziegler's research is challenging. Needless to say, their findings did not remain unchallenged for long. However, they would appear to offer a better tentative explanation for the higher homicide rates in capital punishment states than that offered by the counter-deterrence theory.

Summary: Capital Punishment and Marginal Deterrence

The foregoing review has attempted to fairly represent the various kinds of deterrence studies conducted on capital punishment in the United States over the past several decades. It also attempted to cover dissident as well as mainstream views. Deterrence studies employing more careful, up-to-date methods were considered alongside the earlier research of Sellin and others. In sum, with very rare exception, there is little or no evidence that the death penalty deters eligible crimes.

Lately, some researchers have considered the deterrence question to be static and secondary. To them the challenge has been to explain why homicide or rape rates have been consisently higher in capital punishment states. Some have responded that capital punishment causes homicide by providing a violent example to individuals or by stimulating the commission of murder as a suicidal act. Others argue that high homicide rates and capital punishment are both results of a third factor, a low value placed on human life. A third possibility—that capital punishment is in retentionist states a desperate, albeit ineffective response to a particularly violent society has not been seriously considered. One is compelled to agree with Zeisel's assessment: it *is* becoming increasingly difficult for reasonable people to justify capital punishment on the grounds that it *may* deter. Nevertheless, there continues to be a widespread, popular belief in its deterrent value. It is unlikely that the public will oppose the death penalty, even if the man in the street were disabused of this belief.

Findings on Deterrence and Society's Obligation

Meanwhile, some learned proponents of the death penalty (notably Ernest van den Haag) continue to place the onus in the debate on the shoulders of opponents. They argue that the values to be weighed are the lives of guilty aggressors against the lives of innocent victims. They have no difficulty in resolving the equation in favor of the death penalty. Opponents of the death penalty assess the priorities quite differently. Even those who have no other moral objections to the death penalty, insist that the punishment must attain some socially valued end that a no less extreme alternative can as effectively accomplish. Given the extremity of the penalty, the state clearly has an obligation to proceed on more than mere supposition. It has a solemn obligation to establish that capital punishment is an effective marginal deterrent. Yet proponents of capital punishment have fallen far short in justifying it as such.

For those of us who oppose the death penalty on other grounds, the failure to confirm its deterrent effects is particularly galling. When we reflect on the irreversible effects of the death penalty and on human fallibility, we are compelled to inquire, "To what end?" A serious risk of executing the wrong person as well as injustices in the criminal justice system are never excusable when the supreme sacrifice is exacted.

It is a calloused society that can so consistently dismiss a broad range of objections to capital punishment at the same time that it chooses to ignore or to rationalize the lack of evidence of deterrent effect. Glaser and Ziegler may or may not have taken a tenable position that a fundamental lack of respect for human life causes both higher homicide rates and a reliance on the death penalty. There is, however, certainly no question that such a disregard for human life is manifested in our *attitudes* toward the death penalty. As Justice Thurgood Marshall implied in his concurring opinion in the *Furman* case, our national orientation to the death penalty does not appear conducive to enlightened public opinion. Public support for capital punishment does not appear to be predicated on factual information regarding its operations or outcome. On the contrary, our continued fascination with the death penalty is indicative of our bent for vengeance or our indifference. In either case, we appear to be a death-centered society; there is no reverence for life.

QUESTIONS FOR REFLECTION AND DISCUSSION

1. How can the fact that homicide rates are invariably higher in capital punishment states be reconciled with the deterrence theory?

2. Does society have the obligation to establish a reasonable probability that punishments actually achieve their purposes, or is it sufficient that a valid purpose exist?

3. Discuss the relationship between the findings of deterrence research and the fairness issue.

4. If you or others whom you know favor the death penalty, would the probability that it fails to be a superior deterrent modify your attitude toward it? Why or why not?

5. Consider this analogy from child rearing. What is the optimal purpose of punishment? (a) to vent anger stimulated by the child's behavior, (b) to directly deter recurrence of the behavior, (c) to affirm the rightness and goodness of the violated behavior norm?

6. Discuss the contention of some opponents of capital punishment that it brutalizes society and leads to the devaluation of human life.

CHAPTER SEVEN

MORALITY AND LAW: SUPREME COURT DECISIONS

Many governors have opposed the death penalty on the grounds that it violated their consciences as private individuals. Edmund G. Brown, Sr. campaigned actively against it during his tenure as governor of California, and his son later opposed it when he assumed that office. The late Michael DiSalle was so disturbed by capital punishment that he eventually wrote a book analyzing a number of cases that he had agonized over in his role as Ohio's chief executive. Even those governors who personally opposed the death penalty felt encumbered by their obligations to carry out the law and the popular will as expressed by the legislature. When they employed their powers to grant executive clemency (primarily through the commutation of sentence), they did so sparingly.

Governors have generally pleaded reluctance to usurp legislative prerogatives. In turn, legislatures have been hypersensitive to public opinion on capital punishment. Even such a traditional abolitionist state as Michigan has experienced a protracted battle on the issue. Oregon, which abolished the death penalty 40 years ago, has experienced considerable agitation in favor of reinstituting it.

The Courts and Minority Rights

When various groups have been unable to secure satisfaction in the other two branches of government, they have turned to the courts. The civil rights movement provides the best example—blacks had their greatest successes in the courts. Modern federal civil rights laws were enacted by the Congress only after NAACP lawyers had fought discrimination cases through the federal system, often up to the Supreme Court itself.

Opponents of capital punishment have been confronted with similar initial resistances in the legislative and executive branches. The recalcitrance of legislators and the ambivalence of even those governors who personally oppose it have required that opponents focus their attack in the courts.

Some have attacked this legal approach as undemocratic by seeking to frustrate the will of the majority. Nationally syndicated columnist William Buckley (*Cincinnati Enquirer,* January 23, 1983) critiques opposition to the death penalty by asserting that "the abolition of capital punishment is *exclusively* the concern of state legislatures and in America the trend is toward the universalization of capital punishment." (Italics added.) In a curious sort of comparison, Buckley notes that more states presently approve of the death penalty than the E.R.A.. The general thrust of Buckley's column is that judicial defenses against the death penalty are unlawful if not downright unconstitutional. Skilled counsel should not be called upon to hold the state to its obligation to prove guilt beyond a reasonable doubt, or to sentence or execute in accord with the law. Nor should individual convicts or abolitionist groups seek to overthrow the death penalty in the judicial review system.

The suggestion that certain matters, including the death penalty, are the exclusive concern of the state legislature, is certainly an oversimplification. The division of powers is not nearly so clear-cut. For example, while presidents do not cast votes in Congress, they do take legislative initiatives, twist arms, etc. Conservatives of Mr. Buckley's ilk have generally preferred to ignore the substantial role of the Supreme Court in making constitutional law, particularly in recent decades when the Court's opinions have been so unpalatable to them. They would prefer to preserve the comfortable fiction that only Congress and three-fourths of the states can make constitutional law. To them, Chief Justice John Marshall and his associates on the Supreme Court were not only wrong but nightmarishly idiosyncratic when they first asserted the right of the Supreme Court to interpret the Constitution (by declaring an act of Congress unconstitutional in the 1803 landmark case of *Marbury* v. *Madison*). On the other hand, the Supreme Court has been "making" constitutional law ever since. Decades of judicial review have elaborated civil rights and civil liberties. Those centuries and decades would seem to commend a slightly more realistic view. It is one thing to deplore court decisions. It is quite another to allow them to stimulate the creation of some ironic pseudotheory of the sovereignty of the legislature and the popular will.

The Courts and Moral Suasion   When we discuss the moral aspects of any issue, we enter the realm of ideals, not necessarily that of reality. What is often a matter of superior power is not necessarily based on moral superiority. Thus, majorities offer no guarantee of rightness or goodness. Even enduring traditional cultural patterns are suspect. Neither the fact that a social pattern *is,* or that a majority endorses it, justifies its existence, a generalization that applies to capital punishment as well.

The shift in arena from the legislative to the judicial by opponents of capital punishment signifies more than a change in strategy. It also means a change in the principles on which the issue is addressed and decided. The power of the court is qualitatively different from that of the executive or legislature. Judicial power does not inhere in the executive's command of armies or the federal police or flow from the wishes of the legislature's constituency. Granted the court is always a political institution, and is more or less subject to political forces from other branches or organized pressure groups, but its power is essentially *moral.* The force of courts (especially the appellate courts) derives from moral suasion and the rule of law. It is to the courts that minorities have always looked for protection against the tyranny of majorities or critical public opinion. The courts are expected to be above public opinion, to withstand the pressures generated by the hysterical overreaction of the moment. Their failure to do so on occasion, or at least their failure to do so in a timely fashion, does not invalidate either the expectation or the principle on which it is predicated.

Relationship Between Morality and Law   In any discussion of Supreme Court decision making, and specifically in regard to the capital punishment issue, it is necessary to keep the foregoing in mind. We go to great extremes to separate the law and morality; especially when the distinction serves our own advantage. Conservative critics of social legislation and certain judicial decisions frequently object that limitations on individual prerogatives amount to unwarranted, futile attempts to legislate private morals. Their response to the 1954 school desegregation decision (*Brown* v. *The Board of Education of Topeka, Kansas*) offers a classic illustration. Conservatives deplored the fact that the Court had overturned the aged precedent of *Plessy* v. *Ferguson* decided in 1896. They also interpreted the Court's action as an attempt to outlaw prejudice and argued that you cannot compel men to love one another by law. Meanwhile liberals retorted that while you may not be able to compel altruism, you can restrict the overt behavior of discrimination that arises from the lack of love. Liberals also rely on the argument that you cannot coerce people into goodness. Thus, laws prohibiting such "victimless" behaviors as prostitution, gambling, pornography, etc. should be deleted from the criminal code. Conservatives *now* respond that such laws are essential to the well-being of the community as well as to individual goodness.

The principle that divides morality and law is a double-edged sword. How we evaluate it depends on whose morality is being legislated—ours or theirs. For there is one inescapable fact related to the matter that no amount of hairsplitting between "private morals" and the rights of others can deflect. The law is inherently moral. It is always concerned with someone's idea of what is *good* and *bad, right* and *wrong*. It is recognized that the specifics of the law are always arguable and that the body of law is only an imperfect attempt to reach the good or the right. The good and the right and justice must exist; such transcendent values are implicit in the concept of the law itself. The law is only a means to those ends; it is not an end unto itself. One need hardly belabor the point in a society whose legal system originated in such fundamental doctrines as the natural rights of man. At the other end of the spectrum is a legal system predicated on the totalitarian belief that civil liberties are only transient and granted as privileges by the state.

It is, of course, the principle which is considered here, not the practice. In practice, the law is not coextensive with the morality of society. Some things that are judged to be immoral are not illegal and vice versa. There may be very sound reasons not to legislate against some "immoral" behaviors, not because society does not have the authority to do so, but legislation produces worse results than the forbidden behavior. As the alcoholic beverage prohibition case illustrated, there may also be very sound, pragmatic reasons not to repress prostitution or some other behaviors. Laws in such areas may be unenforceable because of our own ambivalence about them or because social change has eroded the moral consensus on which they rested. The objective may not justify the expenditure of scarce criminal justice resources. The principle under consideration is still sound: its moral character is a central feature of the law. Goodness, rights, justice are not simply fictions, slogans, or vacant ideals, but enduring, guiding values. They justify the very existence of the law and provide guides for its enactment, enforcement, and adjudication. The de facto arguments of the empiricists, the legal positivists, and legal realists have great merit when addressed to the law in its extant state. For example, what Oliver Wendell Holmes said about the law in his essay, *The Common Law,* undoubtedly holds true: The law, at any given time and in any given place, has much to do with the mores, the political institutions, and even the prejudices of the day. Such arguments do not contradict the fact that in all times and places, people believe in something that transcends, the law itself.

Morality, Law, and Judicial Review   The connection between morality and the law has particular relevance to the judicial review process and the art of constitution-making. Basic moral values are so embedded in legal concepts that they are inescapable in reviewing cases. Thus, Supreme Court justices have written on issues of rights and rightness. On the other hand, terms directly connotative of justice and goodness do not permeate Supreme Court opinions. Instead, the language of the Constitution itself is employed. Justices have written extensively about substantive and procedural due process, equality under law, fundamental fairness, and other terms that indirectly signify justice. Opinions seldom dwell on goodness or badness per se. There is, however, implicit in the Constitution itself, and in its allocation of powers and the law evolved from it, an intention to implement a civil design to promote the good life, about which Aristotle wrote centuries ago.

Justices of the U.S. Supreme Court have reflected on such matters in justifying their positions. They have sought the wellsprings of constitutional law and tried to fathom the parameters of their own roles in interpreting it. Their views have varied considerably. Justice Holmes emphasized the organic theory of the Constitution. He believed that the Constitution adapts to changing circumstances and the needs of time and place.

While Justice Felix Frankfurter was sympathetic to minorities and to individual rights, he nonetheless believed in judicial restraint and "parsimony." In his view, courts should not make policy. They should restrain themselves from interfering with the expression of the popular will through elected legislators and executives, and when called upon to decide cases should do so by invoking as few legal principles as required. Parsimony also required that whenever possible, cases be decided on the basis of the construction of the law itself. The Constitution should be invoked only when other lesser legal principles were insufficient to decide cases.

Unlike Frankfurter, Justice Hugo Black was a judicial activist who believed in a policy-making role for the Supreme Court. The niceties of the distinction between making and interpreting law did not concern Black. Nor was he reluctant to employ the Constitution in an absolute way, particularly in defense of individual rights vis a vis the legislature or executive agents. Black and Frankfurter were alike, however, in their objections to "natural law" interpretations of the Constitution.

Natural law theories hold that positive law (the law of states) ought to be derived from ultimate principles inherent in human nature. Since human nature is unchanging, the law is absolute and immutable and not relative to time and place. The process of determining what is lawful or unlawful is that of discerning human nature and deriving principles of right action from that nature.

Frankfurter and Black strenuously resisted what they perceived to be the efforts of some of their colleagues to interpolate their own personal conceptions of human nature and its dictates into the Constitution. Justice Black is sometimes called a "constitutional realist." For him, the Constitution was what it said it was. He insisted that constitutional law-making involved the adaptation of principles explicitly stated by the Constitution, or implicit in it in relation to particular circumstances of time and place. (It must be noted in fairness to Justice Black that he was able to discern a great deal more in the Constitution and its amendments than many of his colleagues. He was hardly a strict constructionist.)

This brief sampling illustrates that constitutional law-making is neither *automatic* nor *morally unconcerned,* essential points which underlie this and the succeeding chapter. Moreover, judicial philosophies and theories have practical significance. They give rise to constitutional doctrines and standards against which particular cases may be measured. Consider for example the currently much-debated exclusionary rule. The rule was first applied by the Supreme Court against the federal government in the *Weeks* case in 1914, and against the states as a whole in *Mapp* v. *Ohio* in 1961. It forbids the introduction at trial of evidence obtained in violation of Fourth Amendment protections against illegal searches and seizures. The rule is in turn predicated on the rationale that exclusion is a corollary of the Fourth Amendment's protections. Exclusion is necessary to deter law enforcers from abusing their authority and intruding into the privacy of citizens. It has also been argued that exclusion is required by the legal principle that the wrongdoer (including the police officer) ought never to benefit from the product of his own wrongdoing. (At the end of its term in the summer of 1984, the Supreme Court announced certain decisions permitting "good faith" and other exceptions to the exclusionary rule. While civil libertarians see such decisions as eroding the rule, the principle of exclusion remains.)

Morality and law are directly and closely related. In theory, the law and the judicial process are not morally neutral. The law is used to achieve the goal of justice and the maintenance of the "good life." The courts render moral judgments and their power is that of moral suasion. The issue of capital punishment transcends the will of the majority as expressed in public opinion and legislative enactments. There are moral and constitutional dimensions that fall within the provinces of the courts and their responsibility to safeguard minority and individual rights.

Capital Punishment and Cruel and Unusual Punishment

The language of the Eighth Amendment is terse, direct, and unambiguous. It forbids the imposition of cruel and unsual punishments—

period. At the same time, this very directness and brevity necessitates that the courts judge what constitutes cruelty and unusualness. The Supreme Court evolved a number of standards in attempting to do so.

The 1976 capital punishment cases that sought to delineate the constitutionally permissible use of capital punishment, and in effect reinstituted it, have been outlined. The central role played by *Gregg* v. *Georgia* to that end will be recalled. Justice Potter Stewart, writing for the Court, briefly recapitulated the history of the cruel and unusual concept. He recalled that the phrase "first appeared in the English Bill of Rights of 1689." Stewart's opinion goes on to interpret:

> The English version appears to have been directed against punishments unauthorized by statute and beyond the jurisdiction of the sentencing courts, as well as those disproportionate to the offense involved. The American draftsmen who adopted the English phrasing in drafting the Eighth Amendment were primarily concerned, however, with proscribing "torture" and other "barbarous" methods of punishment.

Stewart goes on to note that historically capital punishment cases decided by the U.S. Supreme Court have been concerned with the mode of execution. Executions were not to be carried out in a tortuous or barbarous fashion. To use the language of one test acknowledged by Chief Justice Warren Burger in his dissent in *Furman,* the method of execution could not unnecessarily and wantonly inflict pain. Another standard enumerated by Justice Stewart in *Gregg* is that of proportionality. Recalling the Court's opinion in 1958 in *Trop* v. *Dulles,* Stewart argues that a punishment violates the Eighth Amendment if it is excessive in relationship to the gravity of the crime.

The Court's opinion in the *Gregg* case also recognizes that the definition of what is cruel and unusual is not static. Relevant case law is cited and particular significance is attached to the language of *Weems* v. *U.S.* (1910) and *Trop* v. *Dulles* (1958). In the *Weems* case, the Supreme Court's opinion declared that to be vital a principle must be capable of wider application than the mischief that gives rise to it, that is, it must be applicable beyond the scope of the torturousness or the barbarity of the means of punishment. It also asserted the clause forbidding cruel and unusual punishment "is not fastened to the absolute but may acquire meaning as public opinion becomes enlightened to humane justice." This phrase was viewed as a crucial one by Justice Thurgood Marshall in his concurrence in striking down the Georgia death penalty law in the *Furman* case. In *Trop* v. *Dulles*, Chief Justice Warren reaffirmed that the Eighth Amendment "must draw its meaning from the evolving standards of decency that mark the progress of a maturing society." Warren's opinion also insisted that a penalty must accord " with the dignity of man," and must not be out of proportion to the seriousness of the crime.

It is time to pause and sort out the cruel and unusual standards evolved by the Court and to apply them to the capital punishment issue. First, a punishment may not affront the dignity of man. It may not unnecessarily and wantonly inflict pain, that is, it may not be torturous or barbarous. Moreover, it may not be disproportionately severe in relationship to the crime. Beyond these limits, the justices are not to subjectively judge what is cruel and unusual. That judgment is apparently tied to "objective indicia" (Stewart in *Gregg*) which reflect the public attitude toward a given sanction.

Capital Punishment and Cruel and Unusual Criteria

In *Gregg*, Stewart expressly denies that capital punishment is inherently cruel and unusual. He cites its lengthy use in both England and the United States. He also recalls the historic posture of the Court to substantiate his contention. Five justices of the Supreme Court (including Stewart), were able to reach a single common denominator. They concluded that only the existing patterns in the operation of the death penalty were cruel and unusual. No decisive number was ever mustered to defeat it on the grounds of *inherent* cruelty and unusualness. So capital punishment may meet Eighth Amendment standards. It is not repugnant to human dignity. As executed today, it does not inflict pain unnecessarily or wantonly. Nor is it disproportionate to a limited number of crimes such as aggravated murder. Finally, capital punishment is not disqualified by "evolving standards of decency that mark the progress of a maturing society."

Justice Stewart goes to some length to establish that capital punishment is not precluded on these last grounds. He notes that in the *Furman* case, only two justices had accepted the argument that standards of decency had evolved to the point that they had invalidated the death penalty. He goes on to recall the debate about the morality and utility of the death penalty dating back to the nineteenth century. Nevertheless, "it is now evident that a large proportion of the American society continue to regard it as an appropriate and necessary criminal sanction." Stewart noted that in the interim between *Furman* and *Gregg* at least 35 states and the federal government had vigorously responded to *Furman's* emasculation of death penalty laws. He takes this legislative vigor to be a further sign of the acceptability of the death penalty to the conscience of the community. Finally, as noted earlier, Stewart needs to find a way to square infrequency with the cruel and *unusual* provision, and the rare application of the death penalty with the argument that the community accepts it. He sees the reluctance of juries to impose it to be the result of civilizing influences. Reluctance results from humane feelings that the most irrevocable of sanctions should be reserved for a number of extreme cases. Stewart explicitly denies that the restricted use of capital punishment by jurors indicates any rejection of the death penalty.

Public Opinion and Evolving Standards of Decency

The general tenor of Stewart's argument is confirmed by recent public opinion polls. At present, American public opinion does *not* reflect any evolving standard of decency negatory of capital punishment. The death penalty has been the subject of numerous major polls conducted by several survey organizations over the past several decades. It has not exhibited any uniform trend over that time. The polls reveal periodic reverses during intervals of several decades. The Gallup Poll indicated a 30-year decline in the favorability of capital punishment. By 1966, only 42 percent favored the death penalty. A scant two years later, however, the percentage of favoring poll respondents increased dramatically to 51 percent. By 1973 the Harris poll reported that 59 percent of their participants favored capital punishment. Recent polls continue to reflect the renewed interest in the death penalty, with as many as 75 percent favoring it.

Interpreting Public Opinion Polls   Many students of capital punishment complain about the difficulty of interpreting the significance of major poll results. What exactly do they tell us about the American orientation to the death penalty? It is certainly evident that there is a renewed interest in it. The finer dimensions of that interest are not at all clear. To begin with, the national polls generally deal only with the offense of murder. They almost always rely on broadly phrased questions. Only the 1973 Harris Poll had any degree of depth. It asked respondents to select capital punishment for any among six crimes: murder, skyjacking, rape, mugging, bank robbery, and the killing of a police officer or prison guard. While 59 percent of the sample indicated favorability to the death penalty, there was little agreement about when to apply it. Only the offense of killing a police officer or prison guard could garner as much as 41 percent support for the death penalty. Even larger proportions of the sample could not support the death penalty for the other five offense categories. Obviously, such detailed findings are quite at variance with the flat conclusion that 59 percent of the poll sample favored the death penalty.

Most opinion polls on the capital punishment issue restrict themselves to measuring only one parameter of opinion and are content with determining only the *direction* of an opinion. For example, is a respondent for or against a particular policy, position, or candidate? There are, however, two other important, albeit more difficult to measure ingredients of public opinion. First, it is legitimate to ask about the intensity with which an opinion is held. Is it strongly endorsed, does the person merely feel obligated to have an opinion, or does he verge on indifference? The strength of an opinion is an indicator of the level of commitment of the holder. It is also related to the third parameter of public opinion, action orientation. Individuals who hold opinions more strongly are more likely to act on them than others who are less involved emotionally and intellectually. The relationship is far from perfect, but holds. Pre-election polling provides a convenient example. In polling preferences for particular candidates for public office, it is not sufficient to know only who is favored by respondents. It is also important to know how likely or unlikely the respondent is to change his mind. It is also important to know whether or not he or she feels intensely enough to bother to vote at all.

The gross results of capital punishment opinion polls fail to answer such questions. They make it difficult to assess in any definitive way just how significant the results are or what they mean. Often the polls do not tell us very much about a number of vital considerations: Who favored the death penalty? The older or younger? The better or less well educated? Lower- or middle-class persons? Blacks or whites? How intensely did favorable respondents actually feel about the death penalty? For what reasons did they favor or oppose it? If personally confronted by the issue at close range, would the respondent act on his opinion? Students of capital punishment have often observed that the degree of approval or disapproval is roughly relative to the distance one has to it. Reference was made earlier to the opposition of Wardens Duffy and Lawes. An attempt to restore the death penalty in Great Britain in 1983 affords another illustration. When the House of Commons soundly defeated the proposed capital punishment legislation, among those opposing groups who rejoiced were prison wardens and several former executioners.

Justice Marshall's Position on Public Opinion   The foregoing considerations bear directly on one of Justice Thurgood Marshall's central arguments in *Furman* v. *Georgia*. Most of the justices recognized in *Furman* that there was general public support for capital punishment. Public opinion polls and legislative actions both supported that view. Only Justice Marshall analyzed the significance of that fact to any degree. He imposed limitations on the use of public opinion as a test of evolving standards of decency in a maturing society. In order to satisfy the constitutional requirement, public opinion must, in Justice Marshall's view, meet two conditions. First, attitudes must reflect informed judgments about the application and effects of capital punishment. Second, attitudes must not originate in a desire for vengeance or in a belief in retribution. Marshall argued that retribution was outdated as a principle of justice. It is incompatible with decent civilized conduct and a spirit of humane justice. Marshall insisted that the harshness of retribution was precisely at the heart of the Eighth Amendment prohibition.

Alternative Approaches to an Evolving Standard   Justice Marshall takes the position that public opinion may not in fact reflect the true evolutionary state of community standards of decency. In distinguishing enlightened public opinion, his argument suggests another test. We ought to be guided by intelligence and core values rather than by ephemeral public expressions subject to the emotionalism of the moment. After all, for several decades prior to 1968, public opinion polls reflected declining favorability to the death penalty. And in that year, a majority of poll respondents actually favored abolition. If raw public opinion data are the standard of evolving public decency in a maturing society, the death penalty was indeed cruel and unusual at that time. Viewed in a broader statistical perspective, the present favorability toward capital punishment may as easily be interpreted as a fluctuation in a long-term trend toward public repudiation of the death penalty. In this respect, it would compare to the post–World War II baby boom that interrupted a historical decline in fertility in America that demographers had been charting for several decades. That possibility combined with deficiencies in measurement and with the "softness" of public opinion under discussion here makes the public opinion test of evolving standards of decency highly suspect.

The evolution of the core values of a society is a more meaningful test of its level of decency. There are numerous widely accepted patterns in contemporary American life that were demanded by core social values, although they initially lacked strong support in public opinion. American race relations offers a case in point. The law's assault on segregation was in advance of the mores of the community. Still, the maintenance of a system of segregation was becoming inconsistent with advanced thinking and the growing idealism of the time. It was apparent that segregation was intellectually indefensible, inhumane, and unjust. Segregation was grossly incompatible with the core values in the American way of life. Desegregation was an idea whose time had come regardless of the public opinion polls. Sometimes public opinion must catch up with the change process. Justice Marshall's argument suggests that the public must become enlightened about the workings and effects of capital punishment. It is also time for the Eighth Amendment to be brought forward to protect individuals against the vindictiveness of others. A transient majority does not justify vengeance in Justice Marshall's view.

Research on the Meaning of Public Opinion   The weight of the evidence is on Justice Marshall's side in interpreting American public opinion on capital punishment. A number of studies reveal that while most proponents of capital punishment believe that it does deter, a sizeable majority of them also support it on retributive grounds.

Studies have also indicated that a large majority of research subjects would continue to support it, even if it *did not* deter! There is some disagreement among researchers about the relative importance of personality characteristics and environmental circumstances (e.g., rising rates of violent crime) in the level of support for the death penalty. A number of studies have indicated that authoritarianism, dogmatism, conservatism, etc. are widely shared among proponents of the death penalty.

A limited amount of research also indicates that proponents of capital punishment are less likely than opponents to be informed about the utilitarian and humanitarian effects of capital punishment. One study by Austin Sarat and Neil Vidmar presents an interesting variation on that theme. They conducted an experiment in Amherst, Massachusetts, in 1975 in which the research consisted of three phases. First, a questionnaire was administered before measuring subjects' knowledge and attitudes about the death penalty. In the second phase, subjects were asked to read two essays on the utilitarian and humanitarian aspects of capital punishment. Finally, a "post-treatment" remeasurement on knowledge and attitudes was taken. The researchers found that knowledge about the operation and effects of capital punishment were enhanced by the essays that produced significant attitudinal changes as well, primarily on utilitarian grounds. Those who were originally opposed to capital punishment were more so at the end of the experiment. Those who were moderately favorable to capital punishment before reading the essays tended to oppose it. Those who had high retribution scores and were most favorable to capital punishment, were most resistant to change. These facts are consistent with findings from other research, notably the 1973 Harris Poll reviewed earlier. The results of the Amherst experiment also tend to bear out Justice Marshall's contention. The current level of support for the death penalty in the polls does not constitute "enlightened" public opinion. These studies indicate that public opinion reflects a lack of understanding of capital punishment and retributive motives.

There is one other attitudinal aspect that ought to be considered here. It has been suggested that the action orientation of public opinion is unclear from the major polls. How strongly do proponents favor capital punishment? How easily might they be induced to abandon their position? While there has not been a great deal of research into the matter, what has been done tends to confirm an oft-stated view of many critics of the death penalty: it is easier to favor capital punishment from afar. The 1973 Harris Poll placed respondents in the hypothetical position of being members of a trial jury. Only 30 percent of them responded that they could always vote for a death sentence in a capital case. This figure contrasts sharply with an overall 59 percent of the sample generally in favor of capital punishment. Other studies indicate that respondents would require considerably more proof to convict in capital cases.

Ambivalence About Death Penalty and Jury Nullification

Such facts are consistent with the phenomenon of jury nullification. It has often been observed that juries will on occasion refuse to convict, despite proof beyond a reasonable doubt, and in the face of contrary instruction from the trial judge. The Supreme Court's action in striking down mandatory death penalty laws in 1976 is relevant here. In *Woodson* v. *North Carolina,* the Supreme Court considered the tendency of juries to nullify whenever they were not permitted the choice of an alternative punishment. Justice Stewart limited the scope of his opinion to the harshness of mandatory death sentences in *Woodson.* Nevertheless, he recognized that nullification was a sign of an evolving standard of decency in a maturing society. Jury nullification is also germane to the discriminatory application of the death penalty discussed above. Defendants who arouse racial or other antipathies are less likely to benefit from nullification.

Attitudes, Opinions, and Actual Behavior

Findings in other areas of social science research bear out the findings of careful studies of opinion polls on the capital punishment issue. Neither attitudes nor what people say they will do are very predictive of actual behavior. For example, a prejudiced person will not necessarily discriminate against members of groups toward whom he harbors bias. Years ago, social psychologist Richard LaPiere performed an interesting experiment that illustrates the point. First, LaPiere accompanied a Chinese-American couple to 251 eating establishments on the West Coast where anti-Oriental feeling had been running high. Only one of the restaurants refused to serve the couple. LaPiere subsequently mailed questionnaires to the same sample. In response, about 90 percent of the restaurants indicated that they would deny service to Chinese-Americans. Their written responses reflect their social attitudes, but their actual behavior reflected situational realities. A person may be afraid to discriminate, feel immediate social pressure not to do so, or it may be legally, economically, or otherwise disadvantageous to do so. Conversely, an unprejudiced person may conform to opposite kinds of social pressure or self-interest and discriminate when he judges it wise to do so. Again, it is generally recognized that there is a vast difference between abstract possibilities of acting and real behaviors. It is one thing to have blood-thirsty daydreams or nightmares about doing violence to someone who angers us. It is quite another to actually injure or even murder in flesh and blood reality. In the same way, unless one has thought carefully about the death penalty and confronted it on an emotional level, it is relatively easy to favor it; especially when there are strong emotional stimuli supporting it, such as rising rates of violent crime.

Future Application of the Evolving Standard of Decency

Mr. Justice Marshall has strong well-founded reservations about relying on public opinion to gauge evolving standards of decency. It is unlikely, however, that his arguments will receive a very sympathetic reading from his colleagues on the bench now or in the foreseeable future. His interpretation is the stuff of which judicial activism is made. With the passing from the Court of Chief Justice Earl Warren and Associate Justices Black, Fortas, Goldberg, and Douglas, the old activist bloc is gone. The libertarians who revolutionized our understanding of the Bill of Rights are gone and their active approach is out of date. The effrontery required to stare public opinion in the face and declare it unconstitutional is not characteristic of the present Court, which feels compelled to be restrained and give way to the will of the legislature. It is also unlikely that a Court that is so concerned about the barriers dividing federal and state powers will be so inclined. (See for example, Justice Stewart's opinion for the Court in *Gregg* v. *Georgia*.)

The recent reluctance of the Court to find the death penalty to be cruel and unusual is particularly ironic in the light of its 1958 decision in *Trop* v. *Dulles*. That case, which further developed the standards of decency test of cruel and unusual punishment, reviewed the constitutionality of punishment meted out by a military court martial on conviction for desertion in time of war. The punishment in question was removal of citizenship from a native-born American. The opinion of the Court referred to the psychological distress caused by alienating the person from country, citizenship, and national identity. Their deprivation is a kind of civic and social death, as traumatic as banishment. Biological death would seem to be at least as cruel and unusual.

Summary: Eighth Amendment and the Death Penalty

To date, the Supreme Court has not found capital punishment to be inherently and permanently disabled by the cruel and unusual prohibition of the Eighth Amendment. In the view of the Court, the death penalty is not disqualified by the criteria evolved over the years to test punishment. The methods currently in use are not torturous and barbarous, and do not unnecessarily or wantonly inflict pain. While rape and nonparticipation as an accomplice in felony murder have recently been excluded, death is not excessive for a small number of capital crimes, particularly for aggravated murder. Finally, the Court has found further legitimation for the death penalty in the community's evolving standard of decency. The community's current acceptance of capital punishment is expressed in both public opinion polls and in the legislature's expression of the popular will. On the present Court, only Justices Marshall and Brennan would appear to question the legitimacy of these proofs. A majority of the Court is not inclined to question fluctuations, the intensity level of opinion favorable to the death penalty, its action orientation, or the role played by vindictiveness. Indeed, Justice Stewart specifically endorses the view that while retribution is no longer at the center of the criminal law, neither is it forbidden (opinion of the Court in *Gregg* v. *Georgia*). He goes on to insist that in some cases, capital punishment may be the *only* appropriate response. A majority of the Court is not very likely to look at less vociferous but more valid indicators of the spirit of our time.

Constitutional Lawmaking and Future Possibilities   The bottom line is that no total Eighth Amendment relief from the death penalty is in the offing. The Supreme Court is no more willing to oppose what it perceives to be the popular will than are executives or legislators. Careful study and reflection would urge that the present position of the Court is neither morally or constitutionally correct. A majority of the Supreme Court has always been able to find ways to apply the Constitution on behalf of its own perceptions of the social good. For example, the Court was able to invoke the due process clause of the Fourteenth Amendment to protect corporations from regulation by state legislatures. From the end of the nineteenth century on, the Supreme Court recognized the legal fiction of the "corporate person" to whom due process rights could be extended. In 1937, President Franklin D. Roosevelt expressed his anger about the conservative stance of the Court on social legislation. Roosevelt threatened to "pack" the Supreme Court by getting Congress to expand its numbers. The threat, aided and abetted by Roosevelt's appointment of more liberal justices, changed the Court's direction on social issues. Henceforth, legislation that inhibited corporate prerogatives was much more positively received by the Court. Ironically, the Supreme Court took considerably longer to apply Fourteenth Amendment provisions to the rights of real persons. This was particularly true for the black freedmen whom the post-Civil War Fourteenth Amendment was designed to protect.

Obviously, the foregoing does not suggest that the Court made good law when it contorted the meaning of the Fourteenth Amendment in the interest of corporations. Its perception of the social good would eventually be found wanting. The foregoing only suggests that the Court *can find* a means by which to constitutionally redress moral wrongs, if it has the will to do so, and without twisting and bending the Constitution. In the case of capital punishment, there is substantial reason to presume that ample grounds can be found to declare it cruel and unusual, *per se*. Aside from Justice Marshall's reasoned arguments on an evolving standard of decency, it could be established that capital punishment is inherently cruel and unusual because: (1) it does not serve a valid legislative purpose, or (2) because the delays in execution create cruelty or excessive punishment. Let us consider each in its turn.

It was noted earlier that the death penalty is not relevant to rehabilitative purposes. Nor is it demanded as a means of isolation or incapacitation or to satisfy the order of justice and maintain social solidarity, since life imprisonment would do as well. So too would whatever opportunities that a *live* inmate might have to make partial restitution to survivors of his victim. The failure of our criminal justice system to facilitate this mode of individual responsibility with lifers does not mitigate the potential. This alternative will be discussed further in the concluding chapter. The only legislative purpose that capital punishment might better serve than some alternative is the protection of society through deterrence. As already considered, a substantial body of available evidence strongly suggests that the death penalty does not deter. It could then be reasonably held that it is *per se* cruel and unusual and unconstitutional under the Eighth Amendment.

Others have argued that the death penalty is cruel and unusual because it engenders delays in the execution of sentence. Such delays appear to be inevitable in any legalistic society which is concerned about enduring individual rights. David Pannick argues this position with force in his *Judicial Review of the Death Penalty*. Pannick notes that internationally, constitutional courts have not recognized the unconstitutionality of prolonged delay. Nevertheless, he argues compellingly that they ought to do so. He recalls the notorious case of Willie Francis who was condemned to death by the state of Louisiana. When the state attempted to execute Francis, the electric chair malfunctioned. Francis was returned to his cell and the state subsequently made known its intentions to try again in a few months. In 1947, the U.S. Supreme Court refused to vacate Francis's death sentence on the grounds that a second try at executing him would be cruel and unusual. The Court reasoned that the mechanical failure was accidental and let the state off the hook. There appears to be little question that intended or not, Willie Francis was submitted to an impending execution and that by virtue of the mechanical error, he suffered excruciatingly. To resubmit Francis to the same terrifying prospect is unconscionable. When is enough enough? One would hope that the contemporary Court would find such a "serial execution" to be torturous and barbarous.

More routine kinds of delay present problems that are not as easily resolvable. One can agree with Pannick that delays caused by the condemned's attempts to invoke his constitutional right should never be impeded by the attachment of a punishment. It is never sufficient to argue that one cannot claim cruel and unusual punishment in delays caused by his own legal appeals. At the same time, Pannick's fervent argument that lengthy delays constitute unconstitutional cruelty is not likely to be very convincing. There has been little scientific research into the personal consequences of prolonged delay and languishment on death row. The minimal evidence that has been produced does not attest to consequences that can be isolated from prior conditions or from the "necessary" pain attached to the fear of execution itself. Certainly, the matter needs extensive, careful investigation. Objective methods may eventually establish grounds for additional constitutional testing on this basis.

Capital Punishment as Cruel and Unusual   There are certainly ample grounds to support the constitutional position that capital punishment is *per se* cruel and unusual. The core values of American society as already applied to questions of group equality and social justice imply that American society has so matured that standards of decency condemn the death penalty, notwithstanding the periodic hysteria of an outraged public and state. The death penalty is also excessive inasmuch as the available evidence contradicts the deterrence rationale. No other legislative purpose is better served by death than by some other less severe alternative. The Supreme Court has been known to change its mind on capital punishment before, not always after the passage of many years. As late as 1971, in *McGautha* v. *California,* the Court explicitly denied that aggravating and mitigating circumstances should limit sentencing discretion in capital cases to any extent. Yet, one year later, it made aggravating and mitigating circumstances the centerpiece of its decision in *Furman* v. *Georgia.* The 1976 capital punishment cases confirmed their significance. The turnaround from *McGautha* is not cited to predict similar actions by the present Court. It serves instead to illustrate that there is no inner principle of judicial review that precludes a future change of direction on the inherent cruelty or unusualness of capital punishment.

QUESTIONS FOR REFLECTION AND DISCUSSION

1.   Should governors and other public officials divorce their moral convictions from the positions they take on public issues such as capital punishment?

2.   Does anyone have a right to do anything that is harmful to society?

3.   Discuss the pros and cons of judicial activism and judicial restraint.

4.   Discuss Justice Brennan's position that capital punishment inherently conflicts with human dignity.

5.   Can public opinion be in error? If so, should it be determinant? What role should public opinion play in decision-making in a democratic society?

6.   Consider the Court's opinions relative to cruel and unusual punishment from the *Weems* case forward. Does the Court imply that the standard of public decency will eventually reject capital punishment?

CHAPTER EIGHT

MORALITY AND LAW: ALTERNATIVE CONSTITUTIONAL APPROACHES

Capital punishment is simply immoral. It is not necessary to appeal to scripture or to some esoteric oriental philosophy to justify the conclusion. Nor does the conclusion rest upon the humanitarian arguments so despised by those proponents who characterize them as "knee-jerk" or "bleeding heart." The conclusion that capital punishment is immoral rests on a true blue (indeed red, white, and blue) super-American premise. We need look no further than the core of American values to resolve the issue. That which is inconsistent with our core of central values is bad, not good; wrong not right; unjust or whatever moral terms are preferred. Capital punishment is all of these because (1) it is an uncivilized and unusual punishment; (2) it serves no valid legislative purpose; (3) it is imposed on innocent as well as guilty people; and (4) it is almost always inflicted upon lower-class and minority persons. For reasons already discussed, it is unlikely that the death penalty will ever be utilized in any markedly different way.

Its injustice is no less because it is unintended. The essential question is then relatively simple: Can that which is patently unjust or immoral be constitutional? Can the poor and minority person be indirectly disadvantaged by the operation of the legal system, and if so, to what extent?

The U.S. Supreme Court has declared death to be an excessive penalty for rape and for indirect or nonparticipating accomplices in felony murders. Aside from this principle of proportionality, however, their major concern has been with arbitrariness in the administration of the death penalty. The Court has reasoned that arbitrary imposition constitutes cruel and unusual punishment. The Court has not yet seen fit, however, to declare the death penalty to be cruel and unusual in itself. It is doubtful that the Court has ever been willing to come to grips with the potential of the Eighth Amendment relative to capital punishment, as indicated previously.

Chapter Focus

The Fifth and Fourteenth Amendments may also provide valid grounds for the constitutional prohibition of the death penalty. The due process clause of the Fifth and Fourteenth Amendments and the equal protection clause of the Fourteenth are the present focus of discussion. Discussion here progresses from brief definitions of due process and equal protection through (1) the historical role of the Bill of Rights and the crucial position of the Fourteenth Amendment in American constitutional history; and (2) the significance of due process and its application to capital punishment.

Due Process and Equal Protection

The concluding clause of the Fifth Amendment states ". . . nor [shall any person] be deprived of life, liberty or property without due process of law. . . ." The last clause in Section 1 of the Fourteenth Amendment states, "Nor shall any state deprive any person of life, liberty or property without due process of law, nor deny to any person within its jurisdiction the equal protection of the laws."

Fundamentally, law consists of rules and procedures for the application of standards. Due process may be applied "substantively," i.e., the "fairness" of the rule itself may be questioned. Thus "bills of attainder"—legislative enactments that punished offspring

for the sins of the father by depriving them of their birthrights—
have been judged to be manifestly unfair. So too, have been *ex posto
facto* laws that apply new prohibitions and punishments to persons
who acted before the law was made. Both of these practices were
expressly forbidden in Article I, Section 9 of the U.S. Constitution.
However, due process of law has traditionally emphasized procedural
considerations. As *Cochran's Law Lexicon* observes, the fairness of
such procedures is subject to flexible definition. Concretely, the
fairness of specific procedures is defined by the rights and guarantees
enjoyed by individuals within a political society. Such rights derive
from tradition and other constitutional wellsprings. Courts interpret
such rights and the procedural safeguards present in the foundations
of the legal system, in the rule of law, which expresses the core values
of the system.

The concept of equal protection permits of considerable legal
complexity, but in application it is reasonably comprehensible. States
are required to provide equality before the law for their citizens. The
Supreme Court has often applied the due process and equal protection clauses to capital cases, but only on a case-by-case basis. Perhaps
it is time to look for broader application of the principles which reside
in these provisions. Such a discussion will have considerably more
meaning, however, if it is first placed in the context of the historical
development of the Bill of Rights and efforts to protect the individual
vis a vis the powers of government.

The Evolution of Individual Rights

The Bill of Rights has ancient origins in the Anglo-Saxon legal tradition. The absence of a Bill of Rights from the original Constitution
was a source of great concern to many of the framers. It did not
take long to rectify the omission. In a democratic society, it is
assumed that government represents the interests of the majority.
That is the intention of elections. While the original Constitution
was not unmindful of the rights of minorities (e.g., Article II provides for even very small states to have two seats in the Senate), its
primary concern was with majority interests. The Bill of Rights is
concerned with the protection of minorities as well as individuals.
Cynics may dismiss constitutional rules of law as loopholes or mere
legal technicalities. Civil libertarians see them as indispensable to

individual rights, and to the rule of law itself. It is one thing to argue that capital punishment has merit and should be retained. It is quite another to insist that it is constitutional because it is cast in bronze by the wills of legislatures and the populace. Such a contention is unwarranted by constitutional history.

The first ten amendments or articles were proposed to the states along with two others that failed ratification by the first Congress in 1789. The absence of a Bill of Rights in the original Constitution was of considerable concern to many of the delegates to the Constitutional Convention. James Madison and his colleagues in Congress moved quickly to fill the void. The states ratified in good order with Virginia completing the required three-fourths by ratifying in 1791. The provisions of the Bill of Rights were originally intended to limit the powers of the federal government. By a quirk of federalism, for awhile the states were not governed by the Bill of Rights provisions unless they incorporated them into their own constitutions.

When the Fourteenth Amendment was ratified in 1865, the states and the federal government were obligated by due process requirements under the Constitution. The Fourteenth Amendment due process clause was eventually made to do double duty. Not only did it mean to the states what the Fifth Amendment due process clause meant to the federal government, it also became the vehicle by which the states could be held to most of the other specific guarantees against federal power contained in the Bill of Rights. Utilizing the *substance* (as opposed to the procedural aspect) of due process, the Supreme Court fitfully evolved the doctrine of "incorporation" or "nationalization." This doctrine held that Bill of Rights guarantees may be applied to the states if they were essential to due process. Consider the following illustration. The Fourth Amendment protects individuals from illegal search and seizure. In consequence, the U.S. Supreme Court excluded evidence obtained in violation of the Fourth Amendment from federal trials as early as 1914 in *Weeks* v. *U.S..* However, the states were not bound by the exclusionary rule until 1961, when the Supreme Court nationalized it through the due process clause of the Fourteenth Amendment in *Mapp* v. *Ohio.* The Supreme Court ruled in *Mapp* that violations of the Fourth Amendment were also violations of the Fourteenth. Fair search and seizure procedures are a requirement of due process. Hence, the exclusion of tainted evidence follows logically from Fourteenth Amendment requirements.

The degree to which Bill of Rights guarantees are applicable to the states has been debated. Some have argued for full incorporation or nationalization, others for a selective approach. *De facto,* the interpretation that would appear to have prevailed is the "fundamental fairness doctrine." This holds that if the Supreme Court finds that a given right is essential to fundamental fairness, it is inherent in due process. Therefore, it is applicable to the states as well as to the federal government through the due process clause of the Fourteenth Amendment.

Due Process, Fairness, and Justice

The fundamental fairness approach is useful in understanding the meaning of due process itself. To do justice is to render to each what is his due. Justice without due process would be unthinkable because due process is the legal equivalent of fairness.

Our legal system is adversarial. It emphasizes the protection of the rights of the accused, who may be guilty or innocent. Thus, it places the onus of establishing the guilt of the accused on the state. The individual is not presumed to be guilty or legally bound to establish his innocence. Our moral values do not allow trial by ordeal, fate, inquisition, or by unknown, unconfronted accusers outside public scrutiny. Our moral values do not condone physically or psychologically coerced confessions, hearsay testimony, and so on.

The legal process that is due an individual is subject to interpretation. Interpretation rests on precedents and on the principles of the legal system. Meanwhile, the definition of what is *due* is also subject to evolving standards of fairness. Thus, for example, the Sixth Amendment to the Constitution specifies among other requirements that "in all criminal proceedings, the accused shall enjoy the right to . . . have the Assistance of Counsel for his defense." It was not, however, until one hundred and forty-one years after ratification of the Bill of Rights that indigent defendants were judged to be entitled to representation at public expense. In 1932, the Supreme Court declared in *Powell* v. *Alabama* (the infamous Scotsboro Boys case) that poor defendants were entitled to have counsel provided for them in capital cases. Indigent defendants were still denied publicly provided counsel in non-capital felony cases until *Gideon* v. *Wainwright* was decided in 1963. Finally, in *Argersinger*

v. *Hamlin* (1972), the Supreme Court ruled that indigent defendants were entitled to counsel at public expense even in certain misdemeanor cases. The standard set by Argersinger was that counsel must be provided if there was jeopardy of a loss of liberty. The extension of the right to counsel as an essential ingredient in fair play has not entirely assured equality before the law, but it has come a very long way since the ratification of the Sixth Amendment in 1791.

Capital Punishment, the Rule of Law, and Evolving Standards of Fairness

On purely logical grounds, it is difficult to understand why capital punishment continues to be so resistant to evolving standards of fairness. First, consider the Court's concern about arbitrariness in imposing the death sentence. Arbitrary action is the antithesis of fair play. For example, a card game cannot be played in a fair and orderly fashion if one or more of the players is free to make up the rules or alter them as the game progresses. Arbitrary action violates due process and negates the rule of law. Still, the collective decisions of the Supreme Court to date do not rule out the possibility of arbitrary action in the case of the death penalty. If, as the Court rightly judged in *Furman* and *Gregg,* discretion is the seed of arbitrary action, then arbitrariness is still very much with us. As argued earlier, discretion exists independently of the sentencing authority, both before and after sentence is meted out.

A recent opinion of the U.S. Supreme Court in the *Harris* case inspires increased concern in this area. In deciding a murder case in January 1984, the Court overturned a ruling by the Federal Appeals Court in California requiring "proportionality review of death penalty cases," a process in which state appellate courts compare individual death sentences imposed in the state for similar offenses. Such a procedure is presently required in twenty other death penalty states. The U.S. Supreme Court decision did not disable existing state laws requiring proportionality review. Rather, by a 7 to 2 majority, it simply ruled that such reviews were not required either by its own capital punishment precedents (in *Furman, Gregg,* etc.) or by the Constitution.

A careful reading of Justice Potter Stewart's celebrated opinions in the *Gregg* and *Woodson* cases could lead to a quite different interpretation. In *Gregg,* Stewart accords specific approbation to the Georgia statute's requirement of the review of all death sentences by the State Supreme Court. Stewart acknowledges it as one of the statutory safeguards against arbitrary imposition of the death penalty. He even describes in some detail how trial judges are required to respond to the State Supreme Court through the mechanism of a questionnaire relating to the fairness of procedures, absence of discrimination, etc. He also notes that the Georgia Supreme Court itself is required to justify its affirmation of a death sentence by "reference to similar cases that it has taken into consideration." Again in the *Woodson* case, Stewart specifically cites the lack of this kind of review as a constitutionally disabling feature of North Carolina's mandatory death penalty sentence.

Given these clear statements, it is difficult to understand the Court's inference in *Harris* that proportionality review is not implicit in its own precedents. Those states that rewrote capital punishment laws in the wake of *Gregg* and *Woodson* also read more into those cases than the present Court. A substantial number of such states require proportionality review.

The Court's failure to require states to judicially insure parity among death sentences actually meted out is but one source of arbitrary and discriminatory application of the law. There is another more serious threat to fair application of the law. As noted earlier, there is no process to monitor the lack of proportionality between those convicted of capital crime who do not receive the death penalty and those who do. Given these two areas of gross deficiency, it is impossible to insure that the death penalty is not being employed arbitrarily or discriminatorily. The historical record documents that minority groups and poor people have been victimized by the death penalty. These disparities raise serious questions about equal protection of the laws. The grossness of the disparity between the numbers of blacks and whites executed for rape more than hints that there was some malice in the situation. Moreover, even if we concede for the sake of argument that discrimination is unintended, it is no less reprehensible or less offensive to contemporary standards of fair play, to which our society is committed. In such a society, a pattern that *selects* out who is to live and who is to die at the hands of the state is no more tolerable simply because it is not "systematic" or is unintended.

Capital Punishment and the Purposes of Punishment

Capital punishment is unconstitutional because it lacks a valid legislative purpose. To briefly review, the purposes of punishment are: (1) the protection of society through deterrence or the incapacitation of the offender; (2) the rehabilitation or moral reform of the offender; and (3) the restoration of the order of justice and social solidarity breached by the offender. It was established very early that except for the possibility of deterrence, any purpose of punishment is either not served by the death penalty or could be served as well by some lesser restraint.

Due process requires that laws and punishments not be arbitrary. Therefore, punishments must serve a valid purpose. Moreover, punishments must not place unnecessary restraints on the exercise of personal rights. Consider the constitutional doctrine of the "diminished rights" of inmates in correctional institutions. While inmates' rights are limited by conviction and incarceration, they are not entirely abrogated. To take a specific instance, while inmates' mail may be routinely *searched* to intercept drugs or other contraband, it may be *censored* only for a "compelling state interest." Thus, if information relevant to an escape attempt were communicated in a letter, it could be deleted. If the correctional administrator has no such compelling interest, he has no right to restrain the inmates' First Amendment rights to send and receive communications.

Deterrence and Legislative Purpose

The U.S. Supreme Court has assiduously avoided ruling directly on the deterrent effects of the death penalty. Meanwhile, there is a persistent general assumption that the death penalty does in fact deter. The legislatures in most of the states share the same presumption, although they do so in the face of an appreciable, almost totally consistent body of evidence to the contrary. In reviewing constitutional questions the U.S. Supreme Court has reasonably enough always placed considerable reliance on probabilities. Consider for example, that the Court has permitted arrests and limited searches without warrants on *probable* cause under conditions of exigency. With respect to felony as opposed to misdemeanor offenses, an officer need not have witnessed the crime to arrest or search a suspect without a warrant. It is sufficient that it is probable that a crime has been or is being committed. The probable cause standard long employed by the Court is the "reasonable man" test. Probable cause exists if a reasonable, prudent person would judge in the circumstances that it is probable that a crime has been or is being committed. In *Terry* v. *Ohio,* decided as recently as 1968, the Court even permitted the extension of the "reasonable man" test to "reasonable suspicion." On the grounds of reasonable suspicion, law enforcers may conduct searches of persons, even in the absence of probable cause. Obviously in human affairs there is seldom certainty. The Supreme Court does not require certainty to rule on questions about which uncertainties exist.

The Supreme Court may have its own pragmatic reasons for avoiding the deterrence issue. It may even feel that public opinion and the legislative will are priorities that ought to be served. It is hardly sufficient, however, to dismiss the deterrence questions as Justice Stewart did in *Gregg* v. *Georgia:*

> Statistical attempts to evaluate the worth of the death penalty as a deterrent to crimes by potential offenders have occasioned a great deal of debate. The results simply have been inconclusive.

> Although some of the studies suggest that the death penalty may not function as a significantly greater deterrent than lesser penalties, there is no convincing empirical evidence supporting or refuting this view. We may nevertheless assume safely that there are murderers such as those who act in passion, for whom the threat of death has little or no deterrent effect. But for many others, the death penalty undoubtedly is a significant deterrent. There are carefully contemplated murders, such as murder for hire, where the possible penalty of death may well enter into the cold calculus that precedes the decision to act. And there are some categories of murder, such as murder by a life prisoner, where other sanctions may not be adequate.

Justice Stewart's argument is unconvincing for at least three reasons. First, because he overstates the division of opinion about the empirical data: studies have consistently failed to find any evidence of marginal deterrence in the death penalty. A second objection to Justice Stewart's rationale is that he assumes, for a certain class of murderers, far greater rationality than is characteristic of human behavior. It is simply not the case that almost all of those executed to date were hired killers or killers of prison guards. In general, through June 1984, the twenty post-*Gregg* executees did not meet those qualifications and it is improbable that those criteria will operate in the future. Finally, even if it were conceded hypothetically that people behave as rationally as Justice Stewart assumes, it is unlikely that they would be deterred. There are simply too many improbabilities involved such as the vagaries of the criminal justice system, the appellate process and the guarantees it protects, and underneath it all, ambivalence about the death penalty. Especially in the case of the hired killer, whom Justice Stewart chooses for illustration, deterrence is unlikely; he is a "pro" and in his "cold calculus" preceding the event is prone to conclude that he will not be caught in the first place.

What is of importance is what the Supreme Court *could* do if it chooses to. The preceding chapter suggested Eighth Amendment grounds on which to find capital punishment unconstitutional in and of itself. It would appear that the due process clause of the Fifth or the Fourteenth Amendments also affords ample grounds to do so.

The Equal Protection Clause

Section 1 of the Fourteenth Amendment concludes with the clause that directs that no state shall ". . . deny to any person within its jurisdiction the equal protection of the laws." Equal protection, like due process, was originally intended to guarantee individual rights. The post-Civil War Fourteenth Amendment was particularly solicitous to former slaves who were vulnerable to the reinstitution of less than full equality in social, political, and economic life, although the clause was largely ineffective in protecting those persons for several decades. In the reaction of the post-Reconstruction era, rigid systems of legally mandated segregation grew all over the South. "Jim Crowism"—the erection of separate but equal barriers—was given the Supreme Court's approval in the 1896 case of *Plessy* v. *Ferguson*. The Court rationalized that separate provisions were constitutional as long as they were equal. Such segregation was not only permissible, it could even be compelled and maintained by law. Despite the fact that what was available to blacks was rarely if ever equal, the system remained deeply entrenched for decades. It began to crumble only after the onset of the post-World War II ferment characterized by sit-ins, freedom marches, Martin Luther King, Jr., and NAACP class-action suits.

Ironically the courts have been slow to apply the notion of equality under the law to the criminal justice system itself. As the English legal scholar David Pannick has observed, it has long been accepted by the U.S. Supreme Court that one dimension of the equal protection clause is ". . . that while similar things may be treated similarly, dissimilar things should not be treated similarly." Individual citizens are equal before the law regardless of race, class, sex, religion, etc. Equal protection of the laws also requires that unequals—the intelligent and the feeble-minded, the sane and the insane—be treated differently at law.

Inequalities Before the Law

The major thrust of this book has proceeded from the existence of serious disparities in the treatment accorded the well-off majority and the poor minority groups under the law. Attention has been focused on the legal inequalities that have adversely affected the poor and minorities in the criminal justice system. Legal processes have attempted to abate injustices, but gross inequalities continue to exist. The more that is at stake in the justice system, the more likely the burdens are to fall on the weak and unpopular. This is certainly the case with capital punishment. Mr. Justice Douglas's prime objection to capital punishment in the *Furman* case was that it disproportionately selects out members of such groups. Douglas argued that a law which is not intentionally discriminatory may still be applied in such a manner that it violates equal protection guarantees.

David Pannick quotes Justice Krishna Iyer of the Indian Supreme Court who calls attention to the fact that the death penalty falls almost exclusively on the poor in India, at the same time that corporation executives kill in large numbers by adulteration, smuggling, pollution, etc. and are not sought out by the law. Nor are their corporations put to death under the law. Such comments by a distinguished jurist, nurtured by a culture quite different from our own, are remarkably apropos of our own situation.

Inevitability of Inequalities

The Supreme Court has made admirable efforts to redress the imbalances that exist under the law. As long as human differences exist and continue to be mirrored in social and economic class divisions, the justice system will be affected by them. Such would be the case even if legislative bodies were entirely impartial, without self-interest and vigilant. The rule of law is a guiding principle but it is not a practical reality. Justice Powell was quite correct when he wrote in his dissenting opinion in *Furman* that the disproportionate burdens inflicted on the poor and blacks by capital punishment was a tragic by-product of the realities of social life. He argued that:

> The basic problem results not from the penalties imposed on criminal conduct, but from social and economic factors that have plagued humanity since the beginning of recorded history, frustrating all attempts to create in any country at any time the perfect society in which there are no "poor," no "minorities" and no "underprivileged." The causes underlying this problem are unrelated to the constitutional issues before this court.

Justice Powell implies that there is no remedying this situation this side of Utopia. Where Justice Powell errs is in his fatalistic acceptance of the status quo. There is no reason to assume that we have already done our best to improve the order of justice or to assume that the Constitution is applicable only to *causes* and not to *effects*. Nor should social and distributive justice be dismissed as matters to which the Constitution is indifferent.

Given the awfulness of the death penalty, Justice Powell's interpretation is insensitive and borders on cynical. If we concede that injustice is a "tragic by-product" of social and economic inequalities, then we are morally bound to do something about it. We can attempt to alter the social and economic order that is fundamental to so many of our problems; we can alter the criminal justice system itself; or we can mitigate the harshness of those penalties that fall heaviest on the disadvantaged. What we must never do is merely deplore the disparity, or worse, use it as a rationale for doing nothing.

Implications of the Uniqueness of the Death Penalty

It has been consistently argued here that the death penalty is a distinct case: it is extreme and qualitatively different. It is not simply so many *more* years in the reformatory or penitentiary. It is not so many *more* dollars forfeited to the state. It is not simply *more* loss of good repute by virtue of criminal conviction. Capital punishment vacates the most fundamental right of all—life itself. We expect, therefore, that the inevitable defectiveness of human justice will be forestalled somewhere short of the punishment of death. If inequality in the process of executing people cannot be entirely eliminated, then the rule of law and the Fourteenth Amendment would indicate that we are also *legally* bound not to execute anyone. The Fourteenth Amendment cannot compel us to do more than our best to achieve perfect justice, albeit on an imperfect level. But in the case of the death penalty, our best requires that we eliminate it entirely. It is unfortunate that Justice Powell's regrets about the inevitable inequities in our society did not incline him to that possible solution. It is also most unfortunate that 1 or 5 or even 15 persons per year are selected as sacrificial offerings to whatever of society's needs are perceived to be met by the death penalty.

The qualitatively unique status of capital punishment is not only supported by logic and morality, there are also legal dimensions. The Supreme Court of the United States has consistently recognized that the death penalty is qualitatively different from other punishments. Justices Stewart and Brennan both acknowledged the distinction in their opinions in *Furman* v. *Georgia*. It is unique because it is totally irrevocable, because it rejects the rehabilitation of the offender as a prime purpose of punishment, and because of its "absolute renunciation of all that is embodied in our concept of humanity" (summary by David Pannick in *Judicial Review of the Death Penalty*). Justice Stewart stated the matter cogently in the *Woodson* case: "... the penalty of death is qualitatively different from a sentence of imprisonment, however long. Death, in its finality, differs more from life imprisonment than a 100-year prison term differs from one of only a year or two. . . ." Consequently, the Supreme Court has been especially rigorous in applying due process guarantees in death penalty cases. For example, in *Gardner* v. *Florida* (1977) the Court vacated a death sentence on the grounds that the defendant was denied due process of law. Defense counsel had not been privy to a confidential portion of the investigation ordered by the trial court preliminary to meting out sentence.

Impatience with prolonged delay attendant upon rehearing such cases in the federal courts has characterized recent remarks of Justice Rehnquist. His position has not been typical of the justices sitting on the Court recently. At this point, there are clear indications that the Supreme Court intends to limit legal recourse in death penalty cases by abbreviating the process of appeals to the federal courts, declining to require proportionality reviews, etc. It is still unlikely that the U.S. Supreme Court will ever approach the death penalty as anything but an exception in the full range of punishments. Even those justices who could not disfavor the death penalty constitutionally have generally expressed much ambivalence about it.

Summary: Due Process, Equal Protection, and Capital Punishment

Capital punishment is immoral because it is unjust. It is unjust because it is almost always dealt to those who are least able to defend themselves. Intended or not, the discriminatory effect of capital punishment denies due process of law and equal protection of the law; thus deviating from the rule of law itself. Morally and legally, the death penalty is unique and exceptional and, therefore, existing standards must be more rigorously applied to it. The foundations of law and order and the justice system will not be eroded by recognizing the highly distinctive nature of the death penalty or its constitutional disabilities. The death penalty is not only unjust and immoral, but unconstitutional under the Fifth and Fourteenth Amendments. One day, at least five justices of the Supreme Court may say so. "It is a consummation devoutly to be wished!" As in so many other unpopular causes, relief from the insensitivity of the majority—demonstrated by public opinion and legislative bodies—may unfortunately be long in coming.

QUESTIONS FOR REFLECTION AND DISCUSSION

1.   Discuss the purposes of the Constitution. Does it explicitly or implicitly guarantee justice?

2.   What is the significance of the federal system (as opposed to a unitary government) for capital punishment?

3.   Consider the adversarial approach to justice. What are its implications for the adjudication of capital punishment?

4.   Consider the distinction between "systematic" and "unsystematic" discrimination. If any, what difference should the distinction make relative to capital punishment?

5.   Does the Supreme Court's position on capital punishment rest on a presumption of deterrence? Is the presumption warranted?

6.   Do you agree with Justice Powell's position in *Furman* that there is no remedy for the problem of the disproportion in black/white executions short of Utopia?

CHAPTER NINE

SUMMARY AND CONCLUSION

The argument about capital punishment continues. Temporary remissions are followed by fitful increases in the execution rate. Whatever its pragmatic elements or mode of expression, the debate is essentially philosophical. It expresses a conflict of underlying values. On theological grounds, opponents have characterized capital punishment as un-Christian; they cite New Testament references to charity and mercy in support of their position. Sometimes they call on the Fifth Commandment, which in their view also denies to the state the right to take human life in cold blood. Proponents of the death penalty counter with the Old Testament *lex talionis,* an eye for an eye and a tooth for a tooth. They are satisfied with nothing less than an exact proportionality in capital cases.

Humanitarian arguments are also frequently cited in support of the abolition of capital punishment. The death penalty is brutal and demeaning and dehumanizing no matter what the offense against the community. Proponents of capital punishment are prone to characterize such humanitarian arguments as palpitations of "bleeding hearts." They often express wonderment that such misguided sympathies are not reserved for innocent victims and their survivors. Such theological and humanitarian approaches are profoundly moral. Nevertheless they have failed to convince the Supreme Court of the United States. Analysis of the scriptures permits of too much variation both in interpretation and in application. And in the tragedy of violent crime, there are reasons to feel sympathy for both the offender and for the victim and his or her loved ones.

If the death penalty is legitimated in the name of *justice,* it is precisely on that foundation that it should stand or fall. The critical questions are: What are the legitimate purposes of the death penalty? Does it meet them as assumed, or does it fail to do so? Are there any overriding objections to the death penalty? If so, what alternatives might serve the same ends as well? It is a question of the justice of capital punishment, and justice is a profoundly moral matter.

Fairness and Equality: Prerequisite to Moral Application

Whatever its legitimacy on other grounds, capital punishment cannot be morally acceptable unless it is meted out with scrupulous fairness and equality. Unequal punishment for individuals who are equally guilty of crimes of equal gravity is not scrupulously fair. The reluctance of proponents of capital punishment to acquiesce in this argument is certainly understandable. To do so would be to admit that capital punishment is grossly immoral and untenable. It is the poor and unpopular, particularly minorities, who are finally executed. There is a growing body of evidence that prosecutors, judges, and juries also discriminate in capital punishment cases, depending on the race of the victim. In either case, the imposition of capital punishment differentiates between the value placed on white and black life. It may also very well distingush the values placed on the lives of the poor and the affluent.

Only a reasonable acquaintance with the criminal justice system and with its adversary approach to judicial decision-making is necessary to understand why so "few are chosen." If there were no other reason to reject the death penalty—even if there were much to commend it—this alone should compel people of conscience, whatever their religious persuasions, to condemn it.

Executions of the Innocent

There are, however, other significant reasons to condemn it. There is no absolute guarantee that only the guilty will suffer death at the hands of the community. Bedau's studies and our common observations of miscarriage of justice offer eloquent testimony to the fallibility of any human system of justice. The sacrifice of even a single innocent life is too horrible to contemplate. There is no inherent superior wisdom in either the trial judge or the jury. No appellate process assures perfect safeguards. No amount of chauvinistic patter about the perfection of American institutions can alter the fact that we are concerned with individual human lives and that to err is human.

Capital Punishment and the Purposes of Punishment

When we consider the relationship between morality and the law, capital punishment is not required to fulfill the purposes of punishment, and in some cases, it is clearly inappropriate to them. The death penalty bears no relationship at all to the rehabilitative end of punishment. The restoration of the order of justice does not demand it. The maintenance of social solidarity does not require execution. In fact, the collective will to protect society may be poorly served by capital punishment. The controversy which continually surrounds execution is divisive. Furthermore, the infrequency of executions and the ambivalence surrounding them undercut any educative and reinforcing values that capital punishment might possess. Finally, there is only an *assumption* that the death penalty ought to be an effective marginal deterrent.

The notion of deterrence has a particular allure. Concern for victims and their loved ones, abhorrence of the brutality and senselessness of violent crimes, and outrage at the injustice of it all rightly create an abiding concern about the need and ability of society to protect itself against the predator. As a *special* deterrent, death is the final, albeit not inevitable, solution to the problem presented by the recidivist. In a *general* sense, deterrence is the *hope* that other potential murders will be forestalled by making a dire example of actual murderers. An overwhelming concern about the well-being of innocent members of the community tempts one to admit that whatever its deficiencies, capital punishment would still be tolerable if it were in fact a superior deterrent. At least then the death penalty would be understandable and debatable on pragmatic grounds. But there is *no* evidence that it is a better deterrent than life imprisonment. In fact, the degree to which deterrence researchers have agreed that there is no evidence of a marginally deterrent effect of the death penalty is remarkable.

The rehabilitation of the offender is better served by other options. The restoration of an order of justice and the maintenance of social solidarity do not necessitate death. The life of the offender is a very high price to exact on the mere supposition (in the face of the evidence) that the death penalty better protects society.

Judicial Review in the Future

Two state courts of last resort (in California and Massachusetts) have in recent years found capital punishment to be inherently unconstitutional. The U.S. Supreme Court has failed to do so. Legislative bodies are highly vulnerable to the pressures of public opinion. And public opinion is highly volatile and tends to be overreactive. We have looked to the appellate courts for dispassionate deliberation and for enunciation of the rights of the weak and the unpopular. If the injustice and immorality of capital punishment are ever to be civilly acknowledged, it must be the courts that do so first.

A favorable composition of the Supreme Court in the future may put capital punishment outside constitutional bounds. The justices will not lack sufficient grounds on which to condemn it. Capital punishment could be found to be *per se* cruel and unusual and thus in violation of the Eighth Amendment on any one of three grounds: (1) the death penalty is repugnant to an enlightened standard of decency in a mature society; (2) given the current evidence, capital punishment does not appear to deter and thus serves no apparent legislative purpose; and (3) protracted delays in executions are the norm and are extremely cruel and punitive.

There are also ample grounds on which to find the death penalty inherently unconstitutional under the Fifth and Fourteenth Amendments. Ironically, the very genius of the adversary system is also its Achilles heel. On the one hand, the burden of proof is placed upon the accuser and the accused is accorded the right to defend himself should he choose to do so. On the other hand, one's ability to compel the state to establish guilt fairly, beyond a reasonable doubt, is dependent upon the ability to pay for a lawyer as well as related services, in which case the poor are seriously disadvantaged. The dispossessed and the unpopular lack status and connections in the community. They are also prone to generate hostility or at best, fail to elicit sympathy. This is a crucial factor, since prosecutors still retain enormous discretion. No set of legislative guidelines can guard against judges or juries weighing evidence without certain predispositions to sympathy or prejudice for the defendant. And so the few are chosen. And they are very few indeed—the Supreme Court's conclusion that the death penalty is not unusual notwithstanding.

The discriminatory process of social and judicial selection, based on the race and class of the offender or the victim, surely must violate due process and equal protection. The Supreme Court has consistently acknowledged that the penalty of death is to be considered an exception at law. We cannot totally abandon judgment and punishment because the process is flawed. But we can certainly abandon capital punishment because the selection process is so seriously flawed. Perfect justice is predicated on a genuinely egalitarian society, beyond the fondest dreams of the most avid Marxist. Justices of the Supreme Court on both sides of the issue acknowledge that the justice system falls far short of Utopia, and sadly they have been unwilling to recognize that the solution to the problem requires more than legislative guidelines.

Alternatives to the Death Penalty

Life imprisonment is the alternative to the death penalty that is generally proposed. However, the degree to which it incapacitates and penalizes the offender may differ greatly. A life sentence may be imposed with no possibility of parole, or the minimum eligibility date for parole might be set at various durations of incarceration. Generally, life sentences are currently imposed for periods considerably short of the actual life span.

Some opponents of capital punishment do not consider this a problem. They have argued (1) there is little evidence that life sentences without possibility of parole or with prolonged periods of incarceration before parole provide superior deterrence over life terms with earlier parole eligibility dates, and (2) evidence indicates that convicted murderers are statistically better parole risks than most other classes of offenders. Therefore, they argue, permanent or prolonged incapacitation of the typical capital offender does not better protect the community.

Each of these contentions raises serious questions. In regard to the first, there does not appear to be any real evidence on the general deterrent effects of life sentences with or without parole or with varying minimum eligibility dates. There must, however, be some breaking point, some lower limit beneath which deterrent force is lessened or lost. For instance, a life sentence with a thirty-year minimum sentence probably deters better than a life sentence with an 8-year minimum.

The second argument, that murderers are very good parole risks, appears at first glance to have some merit. Incapacitation is a central purpose of punishment, but why incapacitate permanently or for a prolonged period if it is not necessary to do so? This argument, however, ignores another very important purpose of punishment, which is to serve the needs of justice and community solidarity. These require that there be a substantial proportionality between the crime and the punishment. Aggravated or first degree murder is a very serious offense and, independent of other considerations, merits a severe penalty. Moreover, the community expects that the murderer will be severely punished. It is necessary to balance the interests of general deterrence, incapacitation, and justice and community solidarity. The failure to do so imparts an aura of unreality to arguments for abolition and does not serve the cause. It undercuts efforts to reason with many who would otherwise be convinced of the wrongness of the death penalty.

Finally, actual life imprisonment, or at least prolonged incarceration for capital offenses, meets one other requirement. Reforms in punishment and the criminal justice system rest ultimately on the principle of proportionality between the crime and the punishment.

Abolition of the Death Penalty and Related Penal Reforms

Generally American society is overpunitive in its approach to relatively minor crime and underprotective of the community in responding to violent crime. We divert precious criminal justice resources to deal with victimless crimes such as prostitution and pornography. We are also among the leaders of those nations that incarcerate too many people for too long for petty property crimes. Consequently, we lack the resources to deal with violent offenders in any effective manner. We also lack the space necessary to take the truly violent offender off the street for any prolonged period of time, even if the statutes demanded it. Our overreaction to "crime in the streets," and the moralism attendant upon it, defeats any rational ordering of criminal justice priorities. The result is that we exaggerate property values, inadvertently trivializing human safety. Compare, for example, our frequently harsh response to property crimes with our almost total unconcern, until recently, about drunken driving. The result of our skewed criminal justice priorities is that even felony murderers can cop a plea to a reduced charge of homicide and be back on the streets in just a few years. Justice and regard for the value of human life would appear to demand more, independent of whatever pragmatic values might be served by alternatives to the death penalty.

Such considerations ought to be carefully weighed in seeking an effective, just alternative to the death penalty for aggravated murder. Penalties for all violent and nonviolent crimes should be reevaluated and reordered in relationship to gravity and the degree of harm inflicted. Provision should always be made for the consideration of aggravating and mitigating circumstances, and the principle of proportionality should order offense categories. The rational reorganization of the criminal code in this manner serves the interests of justice. Moreover, it is also a highly practical approach to the allocation of limited resources in a criminal justice system which is presently in danger of being overwhelmed by the volume of crimes with which it must contend.

Positive Values of Life Imprisonment

Prolonged incarceration under a life sentence offers certain positive advantages not afforded by capital punishment: the potential for rehabilitation or moral reform of the offender, and an opportunity for the offender to make restitution to the survivors of victims and serve the interests of the community. Requirement of expiation through restitution may be far superior to punishment alone. The solidarity of the community is better served by the positive approach of morally reuniting the offender with the community through reparation than by the negative act of depriving the offender of life. Restitution for crimes against persons is an ancient concept. Its development marked an important stage in the evolution of clan justice. Unfortunately, we have ignored the value of holding the offender directly accountable to his victim or his victim's kin in modern justice systems. Only recently has the idea been reinstituted in innovative programs. In recent years, Minnesota's experiment with restitution and the Christian Legal Society's emphasis on reconciliation between victims and offenders exemplify the underlying philosophy and feasibility of such programs.

Material amends for an awful crime against another person by no means offers a perfect solution. On the other hand, the taking of another life offers no compensation at all. The base satisfaction that may be derived from exacting an eye-for-an-eye devalues human life. The role that restitution might play in personal reform is also a factor worthy of consideration. The offender is forced to confront those most harmed by his action and to recognize the enormity of their loss by his hand. No longer can the offender be absolved of a personal obligation under the aegis of the state, which punishes him on behalf of his victim. Under the present circumstances, victims and their survivors are twice victimized. First, directly by the offender, and second, indirectly by the state, which ignores any responsibility toward them incurred by the offender. Publicly financed programs for the compensation of victims or survivors are inadequate or nonexistent. Even though funding such programs would place an additional burden on already harassed taxpayers, our present approach is hardly just or practical.

Impediments to Implementing Restitution

Implementing a more than token restitution program for capital offenders serving prolonged terms in maximum security has practical problems. There are so many restrictions on the use of inmate labor that it has not been very productive. Profitable private markets have been unavailable to prison industries. Unemployment and underemployment are characteristic of maximum security institutions. Vocational training programs suffer from the lack of meaningful on-the-job experiences. Inmate income is severely limited. There are some signs that inmate labor issues are being rethought today.

Private entrepreneurs are amenable to new forms of cooperative relations with correctional institutions. Innovative programs already underway may demonstrate the possibility of utilizing inmate manpower in more productive, cost-effective ways. In this way, inmates might be able to make restitution while incarcerated, and/or contribute to the cost of their own maintenance, or to the support of their families on the outside who are frequently charges of the welfare system.

There are other ways in which capital offenders could offer partial atonement for their crimes. There is no reason why the talents, skills, and most importantly, the time of inmates could not be utilized philanthropically. They could manufacture and repair toys, repair appliances, clothing, furniture, etc. for organizations supplying needy families. They could voluntarily serve in carefully regulated medical and behavioral research projects. The correctional institution of the future may not be the same counterproductive human warehouse that prevails today. Expert commissions, like the National Advisory Commission on Criminal Justice Standards and Goals, have consistently recommended that the correctional institution should be much smaller and located in larger population centers. Such institutions would be able to utilize existing community services and enable more effective integration between the institution and the community. The opportunity for inmates to engage in supervised community services would then be greatly enhanced. There is some evidence that a few state corrections planners have finally begun to move in that direction. Perhaps it would not be all that difficult to compel the lifer to be a productive human person under those circumstances.

Enlightened Society and Life Imprisonment

In the final analysis, the issue of the death penalty is linked to the fundamental matter of the kind of society in which we wish to live. The final solution of death is too pat a solution to the problems presented by violent crime. We ought to be wary of easy solutions to problems, particularly when they are utterly final. It is all too easy to kill—the trees for another concrete roadway; the animal for its teeth or pelt; the enemy, the fetus, the aged, the defective—and the killer himself. We ought to guard against the growth of callouses on our souls, and against the almost unconscious growth of a mentality which sees the destruction of life as the solution to any problem, including that of violence itself. It is too simplistic, for example, to distinguish between the quality of life and an abundance of life and thereby justify the destruction of life. It is also too easy to play the omniscient role of God, and judge who merits killing and who should be spared.

Society's Violence and Violence in Society   Surely, there is some truth in the contention that society begets violence when it cold-bloodedly engages in violence. Capital punishment exemplifies violent methods of problem-solving. Whether it instigates, reinforces, or merely expresses violence, capital punishment fosters the growth of mutual fears and hostilities and lusts for vengeance. Capital punishment, like war, is a mean business, and it would hardly be surprising if it too inspires meanness. Perhaps it is naive or visionary to hope for an end to warfare. But we can end capital punishment. It has been done before and abolition has not resulted in cataclysmic effects. With the abolition of capital punishment in France in 1981, the United States became virtually the only Western democracy to retain the death penalty. Great Britain, which had in essence abolished it in 1965, debated its restoration in 1983. Despite advocacy of capital punishment by the Thatcher government and a majority of conservative MPs, the House of Commons soundly defeated the proposed legislation. On the other hand, except for Albania, every nation in the Soviet orbit has retained the death penalty. According to William Quillen, writing in the *American Journal of Criminal Law* in 1977, the Soviet Union retains the death penalty for 35 distinct offenses. Earlier reference has already been made to China's recent massive employment of capital punishment.

Dehumanization and the Death Penalty   There is a crying need in modern societies to be especially reverent about human life. Our capacities to diminish as well as destroy life are so great. The scientific-technological ethos of our time has taken much of the mystery and awe out of our outlook on life. Our ability to exert broadening control over the environment has too often led us to view the material world with indifference or as an object to be used with contempt. We have little reluctance to shamefully exploit it and abuse it. An ability to emulate human physical and mental activities through machines, computers, and robots decreases the distance between the maker and the made. The consequences are far-reaching and sometimes subtle. There is the stunting of human potential by assembly line labor where human robots perform routine, repetitive functions in the mass production of goods. There is the growth of a pervasive mental set which subverts personhood by identifying people with objects.

An era of astounding biological discovery holds potential for great evil as well as great good. There is an increasing ability to genetically engineer, to fertilize ova in vitro, to clone life forms—even to create life itself. Such potentialities are fraught with moral dilemmas. There is always the danger that the ability to examine and control life in more minute detail will diminish that which is essentially human about it.

Finally, in a curious paradoxical way, the ability to prolong one's own life expectancy may also serve to diminish regard for human life. Abundant life is less self-conscious, less aware of the value of life. Increased life expectancy is also a part of the overall control that the human species has come to exert over its own destiny. Without control, there was wonder and admiration in the face of nature and in the mystery of life.

When there is an abundance of life, when there is increasing mastery over life, when there is the increasing ability to destroy life, there is the tendency to lose sight of the significance of a single person. Not all things that are possible are necessarily good. While science and technology offer potential for the enhancement of human values, they have delivered little positive solutions to persistent moral dilemmas. There is considerable room to argue that they have assisted in dehumanizing as well as in humanizing our way of life. For example, as already argued, it is delusional to conclude that lethal injection somehow humanizes death. It is only another instance of technological sugar-coating. It is one thing to invent more humane ways to eradicate unwanted animals. It is quite another to deliberately and cold-bloodedly inflict death on another human being.

The social and economic environment in which crime flourishes is not offered as an excuse for violent crime. It is a fact of life. That admission should not excuse our unwillingness to humanize the justice system so that it renders justice. Poor and minority persons ought not to be required to endure the double punishment of economic deprivation and social isolation, disproportionately stringent punishments when they offend against the social order. They ought not to be absolved, but they ought not to be offered to appease the angry gods of justice and society's perception of its needs to be protected.

Few Are Chosen

It has been estimated that of the total number of murders committed in this country in 1982, roughly 2000, or 10 percent of the total, would qualify for the death penalty under current laws (*Time,* January 24, 1983). Yet through June 1984, we have executed only 20 individuals in the last seven and a half years. Nowhere near 10 percent or 2000 executions per year ever occurred. Indeed, so very few are chosen! We ought to ask ourselves, why this very particular few? What rare combinations of personal qualities and circumstances dictates who shall die? If we are honest, when we have found the answer, we shall no longer doubt that capital punishment is unjust and immoral.

QUESTIONS FOR REFLECTION AND DISCUSSION

1.   Explore the suggestion that capital punishment is a qualitatively distinct kind of punishment. What are the implications of that possibility?

2.   Discuss the proposition that restitution is a morally superior aspect of the punishment of crime against the person.

3.   Can the problem of what to do with offenders against the person be considered independently of questions of penal reform?

4.   Discuss the hypothesized interaction between state use of violence and individual acts of violence. Consider the analogy of warfare.

5.   Investigate the post-abolition experience of other western nations. Has social control suffered to any clearly marked degree?

6.   Is there any significance in the fact that fascist and communist governments have relied heavily on the death penalty?

BIBLIOGRAPHIC NOTE

The literature on capital punishment is so extensive, so diverse in approach, level of analysis, etc. that to cite it in near its entirety would require a lengthy volume dedicated exclusively to bibliography. What follows here is a brief, highly selective bibliography that affords the interested, nonspecialized reader a sampling from what is, on the judgment of the author, the best that is available. The omission of any specific source is not intended as a judgment of its quality. Many excellent works were excluded in the interest of economy and out of deference to the nonspecialized reader.

Entries are included if they are cited in brief and not fully identified in the text. They were included to provide ready access to documentation and to properly acknowledge the contributions of authors cited.

Second, significant representations of the historical development or of contemporary thought in relationship to key issues are included. For example, while the literature on deterrence is by no means exhausted, every effort has been made to meet this criterion.

Finally, every effort has been made to select bibliographic entries that represent a diversity of viewpoints on matters where divisions of opinion exist. Any shortcomings in this regard are owing to the breadth of the literature and the author's own limitations, not to his intentions.

The author is indebted to these writers and many others too numerous to list for their research and reflections on capital punishment questions. At the same time, he acknowledges his responsibilities for his own interpretations and for any errors that they may contain.

BIBLIOGRAPHY

Abbot, John. *In the Belly of the Beast: Letters from Prison.* New York: Vintage Books, 1982.

Alston, Jon. "Japanese and American Attitudes Toward the Abolition of Capital Punishment." *Criminology* 14 (1976).

American Civil Liberties Union. *Background Paper on the Supreme Court's Death Penalty Decisions.* New York, 1976.

Amnesty International. *The Death Penalty.* London, 1979.

Anderson, Kurt, *et al.* "An Eye for an Eye." *Time,* January 24, 1983.

Bailey, William C. "Murder and the Death Penalty." *Journal of Criminal Law and Criminology* 25 (September 1974).

——————. "Murder and Capital Punishment." *American Jounral of Orthopsychiatry* 45 (1976).

——————. "Rape and the Death Penalty: A Neglected Area of Deterrence Research." In *Capital Punishment in the United States,* edited by Hugo Bedau and Chester Pierce. New York: AMS Press, Inc., 1976.

——————. "Use of the Death Penalty v. Outrage of Murder: Some Additional Evidence and Considerations." *Crime and Delinquency* 22 (1976).

——————. "The Deterrent Effect of the Death Penalty for Murder in California." *Southern California Law Review* 52 (1979).

——————, and Ronald Smith. "Punishment: Its Severity and Certainty." *Journal of Criminal Law, Criminology and Police Science* 63 (September 1972).

Baldus, David C., and James W. Cole. "A Comparison of the Work of Thorstein Sellin and Isaac Ehrlich on the Deterrent Effect of Capital Punishment." *The Yale Law Journal* 85 (1975).

Barnett, Arnold. "Crime and Capital Punishment: Some Recent Studies." *Journal of Criminal Justice* 6 (1978).

Beccaria, Cesare. *On Crime and Punishment.* Indianapolis: Bobbs-Merrill, 1963.

Bedau, Hugo A., ed. *The Death Penalty in America.* New York: Aldine Publishing, 1964.

_____. "Deterrence and the Death Penalty: A Reconsideration." *Journal of Criminal Law and Criminology* 61 (December 1971).

_____. "The Death Penalty in America: Review and Forecast." *Federal Probation* 25 (1971).

Bedau, Hugo A., and Chester Pierce, eds. *Capital Punishment in the United States.* New York: AMS Press Inc., 1976.

Black, Charles. *Capital Punishment: The Inevitability of Caprice and Mistake.* New York: W.W. Norton and Co., Inc., 1974.

Blumstein, Alfred, *et al.,* eds. *Deterrence and Incapacitation: Estimating the Effects of Criminal Sanction on Crime Rates.* Washington, D.C.: National Academy of Sciences, 1978.

Bluestone, Harvey and C. McGahee. "Reaction to Extreme Stress Impending Death by Execution." *American Journal of Psychiatry* 119 (November 1962).

Board of Trustees, NCCD. "Policy Statement on Capital Punishment." *Crime and Delinquency* 10 (2) (1964).

Bowers, William J. *Executions in America.* Lexington, Mass.: D.C. Heath, 1974.

Bowers, William J., and Glenn L. Pierce. "The Illusion of Deterrence: A Critique of Isaac Ehrlich's Research on Capital Punishment." *Yale Law Journal* 85 (1975).

Chambliss, William. "The Deterrent Influences of Punishment." *Crime and Delinquency* 12 (January 1966).

Chessman, Caryl. *Trial by Ordeal.* Englewood Cliffs, N.J.: Prentice-Hall, 1955.

Chiu, Hungdah. "Capital Punishment in Mainland China: A Study of Some Yunan Province Documents." *Journal of Criminal Law and Criminology* 68 (1977).

Coker v. *Georgia,* 433 U.S. 584 (1977).

de la Torre, Ignacio. "The Death Penalty in Current Latin American Law." *International Summaries* 2 (November 1978).

DiSalle, Michael. *The Power of Life and Death.* New York: Random House, 1965.

Ehrlich, Isaac. "The Deterrent Effect of Capital Punishment: A Question of Life or Death." *American Economic Review* 65 (June 1975).

Ellsworth, Phoebe, and Lee Ross. "Public Opinion and Judicial Decision Making: An Example from Research on Capital Punishment." In *Capital Punishment in the United States,* edited by Hugo Bedau and Chester Pierce. New York: AMS Press, Inc., 1976.

Fattah, Ezzat A. "Perception of Violence, Concern About Crime, Fear of Victimization and Attitudes to the Death Penalty." *Canadian Journal of Criminology* 21 (1979).

Forst, Brian E. "The Deterrent Effect of Capital Punishment: A Cross State Analysis of the 1960's." *Minnesota Law Review* 61 (1977).

Furman v. *Georgia,* 408 U.S. 238 (1972).

Gallemore, Johnnie H., and James H. Panton. "Inmate Responses to Lengthy Death Row Confinement." *American Journal of Psychiatry* 129 (1972).

Gelles, Richard J., and Murray A. Strauss. "Family Experience and Public Support of the Death Penalty." *American Journal of Orthopsychiatry* 45 (1975).

Gettinger, Steve. "Death Row in America." *Corrections Magazine* 2 (1976).

Gibbs, Jack. "Crime, Punishment and Deterrence." *Social Science Quarterly* 28 (March 1968).

Gibbs, Jack, and Maynard Erickson. "Capital Punishment and Deterrence Doctrine." In *Capital Punishment in the United States,* edited by Hugo Bedau and Chester Pierce. New York: AMS Press, Inc., 1976.

Gill, Howard. Review of William Bowers's, "Executions in America," in *Crime and Delinquency* 22 1976.

Glaser, Daniel. "A Response to Bailey: More Evidence on Capital Punishment as Correlate of Tolerance for Murder." *Crime and Delinquency* 20 (1974).

Glaser, Daniel, and Max Ziegler. "Use of the Death Penalty v. Outrage at Murder." *Crime and Delinquency* 20 (1974).

Goldberg, Arthur, and Alan Dershowitz. "Declaring the Death Penalty Unconstitutional." *Harvard Law Review* 83 (June 1970).

Gregg v. *Georgia,* 428 U.S. 153 (1976).

Grzeskowiak, Alicja, and Georges Sliwowski. "The Death Penalty in the New Polish Legislation." *International Summaries* 2 (November 1978).

Hahn, Robert G. *Deterrence and the Death Penalty.* Ottawa, Ontario: Decision Dynamics Corporation, 1977.

Hamilton, V. Lee, and Lawrence Rotkin. "Interpreting the Eighth Amendment: Perceived Seriousness of Crime and Severity of Punishment." In *Capital Punishment in the United States,* edited by Hugo Bedau and Chester Pierce. New York: AMS Press, Inc., 1976.

Joyce, James A. *Capital Punishment, A World View.* New York: Grove, 1961.

Jurek v. *Texas,* 428 U.S. 262 (1976).

Jurow, George L. "New Data on the Effects of a Death Qualified Jury on the Guilt Determination Process." *Harvard Law Review* 84 (January 1971).

Kleck, Gary. "Capital Punishment Cases: A Criticism of Judicial Method." *Los Angeles Law Review* 12 (1978).

_____. "Capital Punishment, Gun Ownership and Homicide." *American Journal of Sociology* 84 (1979).

Knorr, Stephen J. "Deterrence and the Death Penalty: A Temporal Cross-Section Approach." *Journal of Criminal Law and Criminology* 70 (1979).

Kohlberg, Lawrence, and Donald Elfenbein. "Moral Judgments about Capital Punishment." *American Journal of Orthopsychiatry* 45 (1975).

Lehtinen, Marlene W. "The Value of Life—An Argument for the Death Penalty." *Crime and Delinquency* 23 (1977).

Lester, David. "Modern Psychological Theories of Punishment and Their Implications for Penology and Corrections." *Corrective and Social Psychiatry* 25 (1979).

Lewis, Peter W. "Killing the Killers: A Post-*Furman* Profile of Florida's Condemned." *Crime and Delinquency* 25 (1979).

Mackey, Phillip. "The Inutility of Mandatory Capital Punishment: An Historical Note." In *Capital Punishment in the United States,* edited by Hugo Bedau and Chester Pierce. New York: AMS Press, Inc., 1976.

Mailer, Norman. *The Executioner's Song.* Boston: Little Brown and Company, 1979.

Mannheim, Karl. "The Capital Punishment Cases: A Criticism of Judicial Method." *Los Angeles Law Review* 12 (1978).

McGautha v. *California,* 402 U.S. 183 (1971).

Meltsner, Michael. *Cruel and Unusual Punishment: The Supreme Court and Capital Punishment.* New York: Random House, 1973.

Menninger, Karl. *The Crime of Punishment.* New York: Viking Press, 1968.

Murton, Tom. "The Treatment of Condemned Prisoners." *Crime and Delinquency* 15 (1969).

NAACP Capital Punishment Project. "Current Fact Sheet." July 1, 1974.

Newman, Graeme. *The Punishment Response.* Philadelphia: Lippincott, 1978.

Pannick, David. *Judicial Review of the Death Penalty.* London: Gerald Duckworth and Co. Ltd., 1982.

Passel, Peter. "The Deterrent Effect of the Death Penalty." *Stanford Law Review* 61 (November 1975).

Passel, Peter, and John Taylor. "The Deterrence Controversy: A Reconsideration of the Times Series Evidence." In *Capital Punishment in the United States,* edited by Hugo Bedau and Chester Pierce. New York: AMS Press, Inc., 1976.

Patrick, Clarence. "The Status of Capital Punishment: A World Perspective." *Journal of Criminal Law, Criminology and Police Science* 56 (December 1965).

Phillips, David P. "The Deterrent Effect of Capital Punishment: New Evidence on an Old Controversy." *American Journal of Sociology* 26 (1980).

Proffit v. *Florida,* 428 U.S. 242 (1976).

Quillen, William. "The Death Penalty in the Soviet Union." *American Journal of Criminal Law* 5 (1977).

Rieber, Frederick C. "Supreme Court Bars Death Penalty as It Is Now Imposed by the States." *American Journal of Corrections* 35 (1973).

Riedel, Marc. "Death Row 1975: A Study of Offenders Sentenced under Post-*Furman* Statutes." *Temple Law Quarterly* 49 (1976).

Roberts v. *Louisiana,* 431 U.S. 633 (1977).

Sarat, Austin, and Neil Vidmar. "Public Opinion and the Eighth Amendment: Testing the Marshall Hypothesis." In *Capital Punishment in the United States,* edited by Hugo Bedau and Chester Pierce. New York: AMS Press, Inc., 1976.

Savey-Casard, M. "Can the Death Penalty Be Replaced?" *International Summaries* 2 (November 1978).

Schuessler, Karl. "The Deterrent Influence of the Death Penalty." *The Annals of the Academy of Political and Social Science* 284 (November 1952).

Sellin, Thorsten. *The Death Penalty.* Philadelphia: The American Law Institute, 1959.

Sellin, Thorstein, ed. *Capital Punishment.* New York: Harper and Row, 1967.

Sherrill, Robert. "Death Row on Trial." *New York Times Magazine,* November 13, 1983.

Smith, Gerald W. "The Value of Life: Arguments Against the Death Penalty. A Reply to Professor Lehtinen." *Crime and Delinquency* 23 (1977).

Solomon, George. "Capital Punishment as Suicide and as Murder." *American Journal of Orthopsychiatry* 45 (1969).

Stanton, John. "Murderers on Parole." *Crime and Delinquency* 15 (1969).

Trilling, Carol Linker. *Homicide and Publicity: A View from the Deterrence Perspective.* Ann Arbor, Mich. Xerox University Microfilms, 1978. Dissertation, State University of New York at Albany.

van den Haag, Ernest. "On Deterrence and the Death Penalty." *Journal of Criminal Law, Criminology and Police Science* 60 (1969).

————————————. *Punishing Criminals: Concerning a Very Old and Painful Question.* New York: Basic Books, 1975.

van den Haag, Ernest, and John P. Conrad. *The Death Penalty: A Debate.* New York: Plenum Press, 1983.

Vidmar, Neil, and Phoebe Ellsworth. "Public Opinion and the Death Penalty." *Stanford Law Review* 26 (June 1974).

von Hirsch, Andrew. *Doing Justice: The Choice of Punishments.* New York: Hill and Wang, 1976.

White, Welsh S. "The Role of the Social Sciences in Determining the Constitutionality of the Death Penalty." In *Capital Punishment in the United States,* edited by Hugo Bedau and Chester Pierce. New York: AMS Press, Inc., 1976.

Wolfgang, Marvin. *Patterns of Criminal Homicide.* New York: John Wiley, 1957.

Wolfgang, Marvin, *et al.* "Comparison of the Executed and the Commuted Among Admissions to Death Row." *Journal of Criminal Law, Criminology and Police Science* 53 (September 1962).

Wolfgang, Marvin, and Marc Riedel. "Rape, Racial Discrimination and the Death Penalty." *The Annals of the Academy of Political and Social Science* 407 (May 1973).

Wolpin, Kenneth L. "Capital Punishment and Homicide in England: A Summary of Results." *American Economic Review* 68 (1978).

Wood, R.W., and N.D. Harrison. "Death by Society." *Quarterly Journal of Corrections* 1 (1977).

Woodson v. *North Carolina,* 428 U.S. 280 (1976).

Zeisel, Hans. "The Deterrent Effect of the Death Penalty: Fact v. Faith." In *The Supreme Court Review 1976,* edited by Phillip Kurland. Chicago: University of Chicago Press, 1977.

Zimring, Franklin E., *et al.* "Punishing Homicide in Philadelphia: Perspectives on the Death Penalty." *University of Chicago Law Review* 43 (1976).

AMENDMENTS
TO THE U.S. CONSTITUTION
RELEVANT TO CAPITAL PUNISHMENT

Amendment 4

The right of the people to be secure in their persons, houses, papers, and effects, against unreasonable searches and seizures, shall not be violated, and no Warrants shall issue, but upon probable cause, supported by Oath or affirmation, and particularly describing the place to be searched, and the persons or things to be seized.

Amendment 5

No person shall be held to answer for a capital, or otherwise infamous crime, unless on a presentment of indictment of a Grand Jury, except in cases arising in the land or naval forces, or in the Militia, when in actual service in time of War or public danger; nor shall any person be subject for the same offence to be twice put in jeopardy of life or limb; nor shall be compelled in any criminal case to be a witness against himself, nor be deprived of life, liberty, or property, without due process of law; nor shall private property be taken for public use, without just compensation.

Amendment 6

In all criminal prosecutions, the accused shall enjoy the right to a speedy and public trial, by an impartial jury of the State and district wherein the crime shall have been committed, which district shall have been previously ascertained by law, and to be informed of the nature and cause of the accusation; to be confronted with the witnesses against him; to have compulsory process for obtaining witnesses in his favor, and to have the Assistance of Counsel for his defence.

Amendment 8

Excessive bail shall not be required, nor excessive fines imposed, nor cruel and unusual punishments inflicted.

Amendment 14

Section 1. All persons born or naturalized in the United States, and subject to the jurisdiction thereof, are citizens of the United States and of the State wherein they reside. No State shall make or enforce any law which shall abridge the privileges or immunities of citizens of the United States, nor shall any State deprive any person of life, liberty, or property, without due process of law; nor deny to any person within its jurisdiction the equal protection of the laws.

INDEX